Louisiana Bicentennial
Reprint Series

Louisiana Bicentennial Reprint Series
JOSEPH G. TREGLE, JR., *General Editor*

The History of Louisiana
translated from the French of M. LePage du Pratz
Joseph G. Tregle, Jr., Editor

The Manhattaner in New Orleans
Or, Phases of "Crescent City" Life
by A. Oakey Hall
Henry A. Kmen, Editor

Norman's New Orleans and Environs
by Benjamin Moore Norman
Matthew J. Schott, Editor

Charlevoix's Louisiana
Selections from the History *and the* Journal
by Pierre F. X. de Charlevoix
Charles E. O'Neill, Editor

The History of Louisiana
by François Barbé-Marbois
E. Wilson Lyon, Editor

New Orleans As It Was
Episodes of Louisiana Life
by Henry C. Castellanos
George F. Reinecke, Editor

The Whip, Hoe, and Sword
Or, The Gulf-Department in '63
by George H. Hepworth
Joe Gray Taylor, Editor

THE WHIP, HOE, AND SWORD

The

WHIP, HOE

and

SWORD

or,

THE GULF-DEPARTMENT IN '63

George H. Hepworth

Edited, with an Introduction,
by Joe Gray Taylor

Published for the
Louisiana American Revolution
Bicentennial Commission
by the
Louisiana State University Press
Baton Rouge and London

A facsimile reproduction of the 1864 edition,
with foreword, introduction, and index added.

080550

LIBRARY OF CONGRESS CATALOGING IN PUBLICATION DATA

Hepworth, George Hughes, 1833–1902.
  The whip, hoe, and sword.

  (Louisiana Bicentennial reprint series)
  Reprint of the 1864 ed. published by Walker,
Wise, Boston, with foreword, introd., and index
added.
    1. United States—History—Civil War, 1861–
1865—Personal narratives. 2. Hepworth, George
Hughes, 1833–1902. 3. Louisiana—History—Civil
War, 1861–1865—Sources. 4. Louisiana—Social
life and customs. I. Taylor, Joe Gray.
II. Louisiana American Revolution Bicentennial
Commission. III. Title. IV. Series.
E510.H48   1979   973.7'81   78–10596
ISBN 0–8071–0490–6

CONTENTS

FOREWORD

HISTORY, it has been said, is written by the victors, a general truth which the long tenure of the Whig tradition in both the United States and Great Britain would seem to certify. But history can be a fickle mistress, and it is sometimes difficult to discern who has indeed been vanquished. Despite the undoubted conquest of the Confederacy by northern arms in the struggle of 1861–1865, the persistence of the romantic notion of a glorious Old South, steeped in gentility and graceful good manners and universally committed to its "peculiar institution," even yet resists the attempts of historians to suggest that not all southerners during the great trial of the sixties were secessionists or dedicated defenders of the institution of slavery in the name of sacred state rights. There are still those who talk of the "needless war" and of a "blundering generation" which allowed it to happen in the absence of any inescapable moral imperative.

For such notions George H. Hepworth would have had nothing but disbelief and scorn. He was, of course, no southerner, but a member of the invading and occupying forces of the United States.

Yet his account of the Louisiana he knew during his service in the Department of the Gulf is a document of immeasurable value. It allows us to balance against old tradition a sharp reminder that Louisiana does not and did not in the 1860s belong only to those of a single persuasion. Nowhere else is the plight of Louisianians who loved the Union or who belonged to its recently liberated freedmen made so graphic as in Hepworth's pages.

His is, of course, no dispassionate and bloodless report. It flames with his own moral and political convictions, and it is therefore likely to offend those who are content to live in the comfort of old certitudes. But if we are to understand the agonies of Reconstruction, if we are to appreciate the forces which have gone into the making of modern Louisiana, it is imperative that we give attention to the scene that Hepworth so vividly recreates. After the passage of more than a hundred years it is certainly time that we do so, if for no other reason than to broaden the possibilities for contemporary young Louisianians who may wish to find role models elsewhere than in the men in gray.

Joe Gray Taylor, professor of history at McNeese State University, is uniquely equipped to introduce and edit this reprinting of Hepworth's work, having already produced the standard studies of slavery and Reconstruction in Louisiana. As always, he brings to a complex and sensitive subject his own gifts of lucidity, compassion, and understanding.

JOSEPH G. TREGLE, JR.

INTRODUCTION

In April of 1862 Admiral David G. Farragut's fleet forced its way past Forts Jackson and St. Philip on the Mississippi, sailed on upstream, and brought New Orleans under its guns. After considerable disorder, the city surrendered, and a Union army under General Benjamin F. Butler occupied New Orleans and both banks of the Mississippi from Baton Rouge to the Gulf of Mexico. Before the end of the year, Union soldiers also occupied the Bayou Lafourche region and the line of the New Orleans, Opelousas, and Great Western Railroad, which extended to Brashear City (now Morgan City) on the Atchafalaya River. General Butler was replaced in late 1862 by General Nathaniel P. Banks. Banks, a Massachusetts politician before the Civil War, was expected to extend the occupation, to put the plantations within the area he controlled back into operation, and, eventually, to restore civil government in Louisiana. Banks devised a much-criticized labor system, under which the blacks on Louisiana plantations (most of the Louisiana parishes controlled by Banks had been specifically excluded from the Emancipation Proclamation) were to work for low wages, but under discipline that did not differ significantly from the prewar system. Eventually Banks put George Hughes Hepworth, the author of *The Whip, Hoe, and Sword,* in charge of this labor system.

Hepworth was born in Boston on February 4, 1833, but he spent much of his boyhood on a farm near Newton, Massachusetts. His father was a native of England, the son of a machinist, and had prospered in the New World. His mother also was of English birth; her brother was William Salter, a fairly well-known painter. When George Hepworth was ten, he went with his family on a lengthy tour of Europe, and he remained a traveler all his life. At twelve, he was back in Boston and was enrolled in the Boston Latin School. As a student he published stories and verses in the *South Boston Gazette*.

Hepworth's parents were Unitarian, and he apparently planned from childhood to become a Unitarian minister. He entered Harvard Divinity School in 1852 and was graduated in 1855. He was soon ordained minister of the Second Congregation Church, Unitarian, in Boston, and filled that pulpit for two years. Then, after a year's graduate work at Harvard Divinity School, he accepted a call to the Church of the Unity, also in Boston; except for absences, he remained in that position for nine years. He was married in 1860 to Adaline A. Drury of Boston.

When the Civil War began, Hepworth was an enthusiastic supporter of the Union cause. In 1862 the 47th Massachusetts Regiment was formed, and the young minister requested and received a nine-month leave of absence from his church so that he might serve as chaplain to this unit. The regiment was ordered to Louisiana, where Hepworth met Banks and was commissioned a first lieutenant in the black 4th Louisiana Guards. He was expected, not to serve with troops, but to oversee the labor program. Both Butler and Banks desired to keep plantation labor in the fields, but Union occupation and emancipation had, for all practical purposes, ended slavery as a labor system in the occupied area and had provided no substitute. Banks wanted to continue sugar production, and he wanted to keep the blacks on the plantations and out of the "contraband camps." These camps were a burden to the Union Army and a deathtrap for many blacks, who encountered diseases to which isolated plantation life had provided no immunity. Unfortunately, Hepworth's record of his observations and conclusions tells us relatively little about the labor system.

Hepworth was not in Louisiana at the time New Orleans fell, and he left a year before Banks' Red River expedition of 1864; still, he was present during exciting times. He accompanied the Union Army on its 1863 march from Brashear City along the Teche and on to Opelousas, and he was on hand for part of the siege of Port Hudson. His role, however, was strictly that of an observer; he had no personal combat role, though he was under fire. His observations of the campaign are interesting, but he makes no important contribution to the military history of the Civil War.

His real contribution consists of his observations and conclusions concerning Louisiana in particular and the South in general. Some of the conclusions are predictable, and not all of them are accurate. Hepworth was a well-educated New England abolitionist with English connections; therefore, his opinion of slavery could hardly be anything except scathing. Because he was an uncompromising Unionist, his regard for the Confederacy and Confederates could not be high; even so, he recognized the valor of the defenders of Port Hudson. The background that made him a relentless opponent of slavery, however, also gave him moments of uneasiness as he worked with black laborers on the plantations. Furthermore, he was young; some of his reactions can only be described as callow. Nevertheless, he had a good eye for humbug, and Louisianians of 1863 afforded him many examples.

Hepworth arrived in Louisiana early in 1863, and he began his new assignment almost immediately. Although he supervised a contract wage system, he had no personal doubt that the best policy would have been to confiscate Rebel plantations and divide the land among the freedmen; but he realized that this was impractical and, in general, he approved of Banks' efforts. He noted that the blacks under the labor system in the New Orleans area were much better off than those around Berwick Bay, where there was no supervision of relations between planters and freedmen.

In Hepworth's chapter on planters and plantations, he concludes, as some scholars have concluded since, that there was no real aristocracy in antebellum Louisiana but rather a planting plutocracy. He found few books in planters' homes, and the few he found were usually, in his opinion, of low quality. As might be expected, he concluded that planters were hypocritical in their attitudes toward free labor as opposed to slavery. Very likely, the planters with whom he discussed the question believed him to be just as hypocritical. Hepworth was not deceived by the patriarchial pretensions of slaveholders. He quickly discovered, as he probably believed already, that the lash was always in the background, even on the plantations where it was seldom used. It does seem a little unfair, however, that when the South was engaged in a desperate war for independence, this brash New Englander should criticize Louisiana planters for lack of patriotism!

Hepworth devotes a long chapter to the ordinary white people of Louisiana, but the reader must remember that his experience was confined almost entirely to the southern part of the state. It is interesting that he found the wealthier Creoles to be the most unregenerate secessionists of all, "the only men in the South willing to sacrifice everything for the cause." Poor Creoles, on the other hand (evidently Hepworth made no distinction between Creoles and Acadians), he found to be not at all fond of the Confederacy. Nonetheless, he regarded them as abysmally ignorant, compared with people of similar degree in New England. One curious passage deals with a people the author calls "Arizonians," apparently a group of outlaws who frequented the swamps and marshes just west of the Atchafalaya. To his New England mind, such a group could exist only in the South, where there was no firm standard of right and where public opinion was not moral or high-toned. Perhaps he had never heard of the Jayhawkers of Kansas and Missouri.

Hepworth did become aware of the reluctance with which the common people of Louisiana fought for and supported the Confederacy, though he may have exaggerated this reluctance. Most of the Rebel soldiers he talked to were deserters from General Richard Taylor's forces or prisoners who had not been at all unwilling to be captured. Many of them were persuaded to enlist in the Union Army. Hepworth noted that many of these "galvanized Yankees" were of Spanish, French, or German birth, and one of the four Union regiments formed of Louisianians contained men of no less than twenty-seven nationalities. One suspects that those who so easily exchanged gray uniforms for blue were, in the main, recent immigrants who had no emotional attachment to either side in the fratricidal conflict.

It is evident from Hepworth's account, however, that by 1863 the average man in south Louisiana had come to look on the struggle as "a rich man's war and a poor man's fight" and that he had had about enough of it.

Hepworth's discussion of the Louisiana Negro is valuable, even though he devotes fourteen pages to ridiculing slavery apologist Dr. Samuel Cartwright's unfortunate contention that the tempter who brought about the fall of man was really not a serpent but a Negro and that the degradation of the black race resulted from this heinous crime. Hepworth concluded as a result of his work under Banks and his participation in the Teche campaign that Louisiana slaves had an intense desire to be free, and there can be no doubt that he was correct in this conclusion. Not only did they desire to be free, but they realized that the Union army was the sword of freedom, and they aided as they could; their determination to be free overcame loyalty to or fear of their masters. This was a simple truth about the Civil War which southerners for generations refused to believe.

The young man from Massachusetts realized that black resistance to slavery had not begun with the war; he understood that occasional acts of violence and frequent running away were forms of resistance. But the fall of New Orleans gave south Louisiana slaves far more hope than they had ever had before. Probably for the first time in their lives they realized that they might do more than just resist slavery, passively or actively, but might actually escape it completely and become free men and women. Hepworth states, and other accounts agree, that the bonds of slavery were loosened for a hundred miles and more from New Orleans when the occupation began, because bondsmen now had a nearby refuge they could seek. As is well known, tens of thousands did seek refuge at New Orleans and at other places occupied by Union forces. Hepworth's answer to the question as to whether blacks were ready for freedom was that they were far more fit to be free than to be slaves. He recognized the ignorance of many plantation field hands, but he could also see that there were some brilliant and well-educated men among the slaves, and a large number of intelligent and competent craftsmen.

As a minister, the author was particularly interested in the religion of the blacks of Louisiana. His description of a religious service at the contraband camp at Carrollton tells as much about the author as about the people he described. He found the apparently spontaneous spiritual, which he called a chant, interminably long; he even described it as weird. He was sensitive enough, however, to perceive the generations of sadness it expressed. The prayer was backed by a chorus, and he interpreted it basically as a prayer for freedom. Of the two preachers he heard, one, who worked himself into an "ecstacy," brought tears of laughter to Hepworth's patronizing Unitarian eyes. The other, whose sermon was more reasoned, the visitor found more satisfying. There is an assumption of superiority in the New Englander's attitude toward black religion, but he recognized that religion as genuine and from the heart.

Hepworth was also convinced that Louisiana blacks would fight if armed and trained. To support his belief, he cited examples of black courage at Port Hudson, called attention to successful slave revolutions in Haiti, and also quoted a number of bellicose remarks by former slaves. He enthusiastically endorsed the idea of enlisting as many black men as possible into the Union Army so that blacks might win their own freedom and the lives of many young white men of the North might be saved. He was scornful of both northerners and southerners who argued against black enlistment, either as a matter of policy or because they believed that blacks would not fight.

In Hepworth's chapter entitled "Characters," he placed the observations that did not fit into his narrative elsewhere. This chapter has relatively little historical significance, but in many respects it is the most interesting of all. In it, he noted that war, with all its horrors, nonetheless tore away the sham from men's personalities and showed them as they really were—a test that only the crucible of battle could administer. Hepworth also discussed the pervasive corruption of the period, from the making of great fortunes through fraudulent contracts to the acceptance of bribes by agents sent to buy horses for the army. He was especially critical of those who traded with the enemy and even more so of the provost marshals who came under the influence of planters and, in Hepworth's opinion, aided ex-masters in the oppression of ex-slaves. Finally, he included some jibes at the "West Point mind," which he found to be intolerably literal and inflexible.

Perhaps the chapter most useful to the Louisiana or Civil War historian is the last, in which Hepworth described his experiences with troops on the Teche and at Port Hudson. He noted that Negroes were eager to give help wherever Union soldiers marched, and he agreed with many others that they provided invaluable information to Union commanders. The slave whom Hepworth saw on these campaigns was not the faithful bondsman of southern myth who kept his master's horses well hidden until the Yankees rode away. He saw the real slave who was eager to show his liberators where stock was concealed. Perhaps unconsciously, Hepworth gave high praise to the fighting ability of those Texas cavalrymen in Taylor's command who opposed the Union advance in the Opelousas area. He was unsparing in his condemnation of Union stragglers who plundered the homes of poor people along the line of march; on the other hand, the plundering of plantations seems to have received his approbation.

Hepworth ends his book with the siege of Port

Hudson, but by the time that bastion fell, he was almost certainly on his way back to Massachusetts. In half a year, however, he had seen much of Louisiana, its people, and the war, but his interest in the struggle certainly did not end. *The Whip, Hoe, and Sword* was published in 1864, and the next year he published one of his sermons as a pamphlet entitled *The Criminal; the Crime; the Penalty*, in which he advocated the summary execution of Jefferson Davis. *Two Sermons*, published the same year, contains a Fourth of July oration and his thoughts on Lincoln's death. Both expressed the unforgiving attitude of ultraradicalism.

During the remainder of his life, Hepworth divided his time between the ministry and journalism. In 1867 he began preaching in a Boston theater in an attempt to reach a larger audience, and he established a short-lived school for the training of missionaries. In 1869 he accepted a call to the Church of the Messiah in New York, and in 1870 he published *Rocks and Shoals: Lectures to Young Men*. In 1873 Hepworth broke with the Unitarians and became pastor of the Congregational Church of the Disciples, which he organized; he remained in its pulpit until 1879. In 1876 he published a book on the art of sailing, entitled *Starboard and Port*. In 1880 he went abroad; this made him available to serve as the United States representative on a committee to disburse funds to the victims of the Irish famine of that year. These funds had been raised by James Gordon Bennett's New York *Herald*.

After his return from Europe, Hepworth accepted the Belleville Avenue Congregational Church pastorate, which he held until 1885. He had come to be a friend of Bennett, however, and it is obvious that he devoted as much time to journalism as to his pastorate, contributing to various periodicals and writing a column for the *Herald*. In 1882 he became one of Bennett's editors, and after 1885, when he could devote full time to the task, he became superintending editor. In 1893 he became chief editor of the New York *Telegram*. During the remainder of his career he published ten more books, most of them inspirational. One, *Hiram Golf's Religion*, sold more than 35,000 copies. His last book, which resulted from a request by Bennett for an investigation of conditions in Armenia, is a travel account, *Through Armenia on Horseback*. Hepworth died on June 7, 1902.

Hepworth was certainly not one of America's great literary figures, and *The Whip, Hoe, and Sword* is not deathless prose. It does have value, however, for it reveals what a well-educated young northerner thought of Louisiana's people and institutions in the midst of the Civil War. Obviously, the book is biased; but it is important to know what men with Hepworth's bias thought, and thus the book has been included in this series of reprints.

THE

WHIP, HOE, AND SWORD;

OR,

THE GULF-DEPARTMENT IN '63.

BY

GEORGE H. HEPWORTH.

"This is all true as it is strange:
Nay, it is ten times true; for truth is truth
To the end of reckoning."
SHAKSPEARE.

BOSTON:

WALKER, WISE, AND COMPANY,

245, WASHINGTON STREET.

1864.

BOSTON:
PRINTED BY JOHN WILSON & SON,
5, WATER STREET.

PREFACE.

My book was written *con amore*, and in the midst of the scenes described. I never journeyed without my note-book and pencil, and was careful to record conversations as soon as possible after their occurrence.

I was with our forces when they marched through the Têche, and when they were before Port Hudson. I have seen our boys under all possible circumstances, — in the camp, on the march, in the field, and in the hospital; and I believe that the world never saw an army its equal in culture, fortitude, and patriotism. There never has been a time in our history, when to be an American citizen or an American soldier could be reckoned so great a privilege as it is to-day.

If I talk a great deal of slavery, it is because I have seen a great deal of it. If I say no good thing of it, it is because I found no good thing in it. I learned to pity the slaveholder and the slave, and to thank God and the genius of the age for the Proclamation.

I have to express my warmest gratitude to Gen. Banks, who kindly allowed me every privilege in my work of investigation, and to whom we are indebted for the successful operation of the free-labor system in the Gulf Department. Let all honor be given to an honorable man.

As my people said to me when I left them, so say I to my book, " God speed you ! "

Boston, Nov. 1863.

CONTENTS.

CHAPTER I.

THE WHIP, HOE, AND SWORD.

CHAPTER I.

GOOD-BY FOR A YEAR.

FROM the very first, I desired to go to the war. I felt that no man has any right to look about him for an excuse to stay at home. If blessed with good health, his first duty is to his country; for, without his country's benignant laws and institutions, he is worth just nothing.

When I looked upon those who had put on the harness, I wanted nothing so much as to go with them; and, when I looked about me on those who remained at home, my desire to go grew apace.

I had often revelled in the rich scenes of the last century, when a lifetime seemed so much; when one generation held in its hands the fate of many ages; and when manly men were building the future, as we build a temple. Those were glorious days, and days in which it was a sublime privilege to live. The rusty sword of the humblest farmer was as much needed as the bright Damas-

cus blade of the leader. Every strong-limbed man
and every tender-hearted woman contributed to
that aggregate force which founded a new empire.
" Will those days ever come again ? " I asked myself each time I laid the record on its shelf.

Then came through our New-England homes the
invigorating reverberations from Sumter. The
trumpet-tongued cannon seemed to thunder forth
the prophecy of a new life. The church-bells
joined in the chorus ; and pulpit and rostrum sent
out their cry, " To arms for Freedom ! " and told
us that the days of chivalry were at hand, and that
every willing knight was needed for the contest.

It mattered not that I was the humblest disciple
of one who came to still the troubled waters, and
to bring peace upon earth. The day had not yet
come when it would be quite safe to give up the
sword for a pruning-hook: on the contrary, our
chief duty seemed to be to change all pruning-
hooks into swords.

So I said to my people, " I can stay no longer ; "
and they kindly answered, " Go, and God speed
you ! "

On the sabbath morning when I reached the top
of the hill that overlooked our camp, the bells
began to ring, summoning the villagers to the
house of God. It seemed to me that they had a
voice, which said, —

"Chaplain, the work before you is hard, but grand. A thousand mothers, wives, and daughters have given those they dearly love for their country. A thousand homes will support your arms, while a thousand altar-fires will burn low for nine long months; and many, alas! will never be kindled into their wonted brilliancy, because there is war, bloody war, in the land. Look to your duty. Pray for the boy, who, until now, has never known temptation; warn the husband and the father who is walking, as fast as he can, in the road that leads to moral death, and who will bring back to his family, at the end of his term of service, a poisoned mind and heart; and when the dark day lowers, and the air is thick with battle-smoke, speak, with the Master's authority, the 'Peace, be still!' to those who have fallen; and open, with the hand of friendship and of prayer, the door of heaven, that they may enter to receive their reward."

All this the many-toned village church-bells rang out; and I trembled as I remembered that all I could offer to my country were willing hands and a willing heart.

We started from Readville at ten minutes past one, P.M. I need not repeat that it was on Sunday; for, as a general thing, our battles have been fought and our movements made on that day. We tried to effect a delay until Monday; but our orders were peremptory, and nothing was left but obedience. Indeed, so imperative were the commands from headquarters, that we made all despatch, under the impression that our services would be required immediately. We had not then been initiated into the jocular ways of Government officials; we did not know that these same officials, who are receiving large salaries, with which they are enabled to exhibit the profundity of their ignorance, oftentimes please themselves by getting our troops into the most delightful snarls, and then allowing them to find their own way out. We were one of the victims of this most fashionable recreation. Hurrying forward with all speed, eager to do our work in the fray, we reached Groton Junction, filed out of the cars, and stood on the wharf, ready to embark on the "Commodore." We strained our eyes with looking, knowing we were needed in New York at once; but no vessel appeared. An hour passed, and another, and still another, till five mortal hours sped on their way; when the steamer rounded leisurely up to the wharf. We reached New York on Monday morning, and our colonel at once reported at headquarters. To our chagrin, the officers of our good Uncle Sam were greatly surprised to see us.

"Did you not distinctly and imperatively order us to start at once?"

" Certainly; but is that any reason why you should do so?"

It was very much like the invitation to dinner which the Chinaman extended to his friend: the friend did not know enough to refuse, and so gave offence to the polite celestial. We were thus let into one of many secrets. We learned, that when Government telegraphs in seemingly great haste, commanding a regiment to move at once, it is only because it is in good-humor, and enjoys a joke. You may hurry as much as you will; you may leave behind many necessary articles which you hoped to carry with you; you may even infuse a good spirit into your men by an exciting and patriotic speech; you may stir them, so that they will give cheer after cheer for the good old flag, and, without knowing it, come to the " Charge bayonet!" yet, after all, this whole experience is to be reckoned among the delusions of war. You will probably lie in barracks for weeks, and not hear the slightest intimation that Government needs you, or even knows of your existence.

On Sunday, the 21st of December, we embarked on the " Mississippi," bound to sea with sealed orders. We were not allowed to open the letter which gave us our destination until we had steamed due south twenty-four hours. We all were hopeful and happy as the head of the vessel

swung round in the Narrows; and we started on
our journey, our hearts keeping time with the
"Hail, Columbia!" of our band. The sun set glo-
riously that afternoon, just as we lost sight of the
great busy city which held many who were very
dear to us; and as we looked forward to the wide
expanse that lay stretched before us, smooth as a
western prairie, I, for the first time, really felt that
I had turned my face from my home.

The next morning, the breakfast-table was not
quite full. There was many a "vacant chair," and
many a lugubrious face. Neptune must be a very
queer individual; for one no sooner looks upon him
than he is attacked with strange sensations, which
seem to have no local habitation, but, Gypsy-like,
wander all over the body from head to foot. The
patient at once loses all esteem of himself, is robbed
of all elasticity, and sinks on his couch, or on
any place that is handy; entertaining the most
extreme disgust for the world, and for every particular individual in it. The disease is attended
with great self-reproach; the patient wondering
that he could ever have been induced to trust
himself in any thing so unstable as a ship; and
inwardly vowing, that if he is permitted to get on
land, even though it be a piece only large enough
to stand upon, he will never again trust himself to
be rocked in the cradle of the deep.

The second day we passed Hatteras, and the sea was as smooth as any landsman could desire. The winds remembered that we were all Union boys, and refused to tempt the ocean's anger. So we sped on our way, each hour bringing us into warmer weather, until, on the fourth day, we caught sight of the Bahamas. After that, the temperature was so inviting, that I took my blanket every night, and made a bed for myself on the deck. On the fifth day, we passed the Florida Keys. These islands, as well as the Bahamas, are only sand-plains, heaped about nuclei of coral; and so low, that one can hardly see them until he comes within four or five miles of them.

We were fortunate enough to have moonlight nights during our whole passage; and it was my delight to sit on the rail of the quarter-deck, and watch the white, sparkling river of foam in which we seemed to be floating. The full moon gave it the appearance of snow, while its own phosphorescence seemed to stud it with brilliant stars. You can hardly imagine any thing more beautiful, — all around you, the smooth black waters of the Gulf; just behind you, and stretching back for a hundred feet or more, a rumbling, tumbling snow-drift, filled with sparkling gems. It was so fascinating, that I used to sit till far into the night, watching its endless changes. Once, I remember, the dolphins played for a while about our ship; and, while they flew along the surface, their back fins cut through the water with such rapidity, that they left a slender line of phosphorescent snow behind them. It seemed to me like a silver line of poetry written on the dark page of the ocean.

We had a delightful time in the Gulf; for all our sea-sickness was gone, and every thing about us was pleasant to behold. We reached Ship Island in seven days and a half; and, having cast anchor, learned that we were to stay just thirty minutes, and then start for New Orleans. The island is a dreary place; only a huge sand-bank, at one end of which is a pond of brackish water filled with alligators; and, at the other end, the beginning of what may, some time, be an impregnable fort. I think, that, even now, no land force could take the work: for, except immediately after a heavy rain, one sinks more than ankle-deep in sand; and, when there is a heavy wind, the hillocks actually change their positions, — the process of emigration filling the air with gritty particles enough to give the whole world the ophthalmia. I have often thought that the topography of the island must be very puzzling to a systematic man. He may labor during the day, and at nightfall every elevation shall be correctly positioned. When the night comes, bringing a strong south-easter, he sleeps with his maps under his head for security.. In the morning, he emerges from his tent, and alternately views his map and the landscape. Some prestidigitateur has been at work. None of the hillocks are where they ought to be. Like an army, they only bivouacked where he found them; since which time, they have seen fit to " change their base." Ship Island is a grand place for one who is disgusted with the world, but a very disagreeable place for one who has any desire to enjoy himself.

We started at four, P.M.; and anchored just off the Bar, in the " Father of Waters," some time the next evening. I was glad of this ; for it gave me an opportunity to see the plantations on each side of the river, of which I had heard so much.

Early in the morning, we entered the Southwest Pass, crossed the Bar, and passed the sunken wreck of the fire-boat which the rebels had set adrift, in hopes thereby to fire Farragut's fleet. It ended its ignoble career as it should; finding a grave in Mississippi mud.

The river presented no objects of interest for many miles; .indeed, not until we reached the Forts St. Philip and Jackson. Jackson is the principal work, situated on the right bank of the river, and almost immediately opposite Fort St. Philip. We saw nothing to remind us of the struggle which gave us New Orleans, except a gunboat or two destroyed during the fight, and driven as high as possible on the bank of the river. Yet, said they who saw the fight, it was a terrible contest. The rebels were fresh, eager for the fray, and reckless in their daring. They believed themselves secure against any attack of the Federals. They had strengthened their fortifications in every possible way, and had mounted guns which have since been proved excellent. A picket-guard had been stationed a couple of miles below to signal the first approach of the enemy. They could commence to fire at our boats when over two miles distant. Besides all this, they had three immense iron cables stretched across the river, to which was attached a bridge ; so that communication between the two forts was complete. If our fleet should succeed in getting opposite the fort, this impediment would bar its further progress ; and, before it could get out of range again, it would be utterly destroyed. But —

   " The best-laid schemes of mice and men gang aft agley."

Our fleet-commander was aware of the existence of this chain, and destroyed it in a very neat way. The water runs, at this point, about three miles an hour. This tremendous pressure brought a great strain against the iron ; and, when the floating-bridge was attached, the current pressed against the immense amount of woodwork, and strained the cable to its utmost. Our commander, knowing this, sent one of his fleetest boats — a boat with an iron prow, and sharp — to stem the current at its utmost speed, and strike the cable in the centre of the river, where the pressure was greatest. The experiment was remarkably successful. The boat hit the chain in just the right place, and it parted as if by magic ; one half the bridge floating to the east side of the river, and the other half to the west side. I have often, when a boy, bent a young tree, half as thick as my arm, almost to the ground, and then, striking it on the upper side where the strain was greatest, cut it completely through with the quick blow of a hatchet. It was in the same way that the great chain was broken.

The fleet of the Union came up the river slowly, — feeling its way along, fearing some infernal machine, — and nothing was heard on that calm but dark night save the striking of their paddles in the water. The decks were filled with men, who expected to pay a heavy price for the victory, and who were willing to give their lives. The pilot, Porter, knew every shoal, every bend, every snag. If anybody could take our fleet by those forts, Porter was the man. I have thought, what an hour of intense excitement that must have been on both sides ! The rebels did not believe that our men would attempt such a hopeless task, yet kept on the alert; and, on that night, trained ears were listening to catch the sound of paddle-wheels, and trained eyes were peering through the darkness. Nobody saw the glorious stars and stripes which were floating to the breeze from the masthead of every gunboat. Nobody saw the stars and bars which were polluting the air above the forts. Soon, however, the terrific conflict between right and wrong began. Our leading gunboats could not have been much more than half a mile distant from the fort, when the battle opened by iron hail from the rebel guns. Our boats did not answer for a while, but kept steadily on, hugging the farther shore. When, however, they were directly opposite Fort St. Philip, their voices were heard; and they poured upon the rebels a rain which they were not prepared for. Still we kept right on; the object being to get by the forts.

What a picture for the historian to draw! The night was so dark, that the rebels could see to fire, only by the flashes from our guns, or perchance by the grim blackness of our gunboats, seen against the lighter background of sky.

I need not say, that our entire fleet got by the forts; and that that night's work opened for us the mouth of the Mississippi, and gave us New Orleans.

As we turned bend after bend in the river, our eyes — alas ! it was only our eyes — were greeted by orange-groves laden with their luscious fruit. All on board played the part of Tantalus : for we thirsted for the delicious drink contained in the yellow spheres ; and it was almost, but not quite, within our reach.

The Mississippi is indeed a mighty and marvellous river. When it rises in the spring, rolling its lordly and muddy flood with the impetuosity of a smaller stream, the planters look carefully to their levees ; for their land, and all their houses, are from five to eight feet below the boiling surface of the water : and when, in the summer, it falls, they must again be vigilant; for it often happens, that the swift current digs out the side of the bank under the levee ; so that, when the water falls, an acre or two will cave in. The river will sometimes rob one planter of twenty acres by compelling him to place his levee two hundred feet back from the bank, and give another planter twenty acres by changing its channel. The Father of Waters is very capricious.

The river at New Orleans rises in the spring thirteen feet from its ordinary level ; at Baton Rouge, it rises about twenty-seven feet ; and, at the mouth of the Ohio, some fifty or sixty feet. The floods at the Yellow Stone make no perceptible change in the river at New Orleans for thirty days after their commencement.

There is one shell-fish which seems to be working in the way. of Providence and the Union so zealously, that he deserves a passing notice. The fiddler resembles a crab, though he is much smaller. He seems to be impressed with the fact, that men have no right to limit the river, by means of levees, to the narrow space between its banks; and, further, that it can help the Federals in overcoming the rebels who live near it. Thus impressed, it works steadily, night and day, boring holes through the Levee. I have seen a levee completely honeycombed by these creatures. They are to be counted by millions; and will dig through an earthwork ten, and even fifteen, feet in thickness. Half the disasters along the river are to be attributed to these little creatures. Verily, the planters are being well punished; for they fear nothing so much as these Union fiddlers.

None of the whites greeted us with a single cheer on our entire river-passage. They only deigned to thrust their hands as deeply as possible into their pockets, and gaze sullenly at us. Why should they be glad to see us? Is the thief, who has stolen goods in his possession, desirous of an intimacy with the sturdy policeman who is on his track? They are the veriest cowards of the

South; men, or rather things in men's clothes, who are too careful of their precious lives to go into the Confederate Army; and so lounge about at home, taking the oath of allegiance with lying lips, and spitting at Union soldiers *behind their backs.*

The blacks alone welcomed us with vociferous shouts and frantic gestures. Whether they knew the deep significance of the day, — the 1st of January, — or not, I cannot say. They gathered, in little companies of ten or twenty, on the bank of the river, and in front of their masters' dwellings; and, as we went by, greeted us with peals of laughter, and cheers for the " Northerners."

That night, we anchored just opposite the lower end of the city. The next morning, we reported at headquarters, were very kindly received by Gen. Banks, and ordered to proceed at once to Carrollton, some fourteen miles up the river; which place we reached in due time.

CHAPTER II.

PLANTERS AND PLANTATIONS.

WHEN I first went to the St. Charles to pay my respects to Gen. Banks, he was kind enough to say that he would be glad to help me in any way I might suggest; and that I might call upon him at any future time, and remind him of his promise. I kept these words in my heart; for I had already begun to feel that my chaplaincy tended to confine rather than give ample scope to my desire for work.

We had been in Carrollton but a few days, when the glad tidings came, "To the front!" but, the very next day, some good excuse was discovered for disobedience; and we immediately began to take root where we were. I afterwards heard, on good authority, that the order had been repeated, and that a second time an excuse had been found. The boys of the regiment were all earnestly sorry. They left their friends with the expectation of doing their part in the general bayonet-exercise; and were loud in their complaints when it was discovered that the colors were to be as fresh and

bright at the end of the nine months as at the
beginning. The staff-officers were so unanimous in
their disapproval of such a " peace policy," that,
in a few weeks, not one was left. Each had succeeded in getting detached, and sent from the city
on special duty.

The truth is, there are some old women in the
army. A pity it is that they cannot be convinced
of their sex!

The moment I saw the actual position of affairs,
and had fully assured myself of the direction
which the current of our fortunes was to take, I
went to Gen. Banks, and reminded him of his promise. He agreed to give me a commission as first
lieutenant in the Fourth Louisiana Native Guards,
and thence detail me as aide-de-camp. This very
kind offer I at once accepted, because it would
give me an honorable position, and afford me ample
opportunity to choose my own fields of labor.

Just at that time, the negro question was pressed
with unusual force upon our attention. Large
numbers of blacks were crowding within our lines,
and Government was issuing to each person about
three-quarters of a ration per day. The children
were dying in frightful numbers; and the general
mortality was such, that the whole subject demanded immediate attention. These people were
living in the most unhealthy localities, and, without

2

doubt, in the most immoral way. They found no work, and were really in a very pitiable condition. The *best* thing to do was to enlist all the able-bodied men, confiscate every plantation in the department, and, dividing land up into twenty-acre lots, give each black family one such lot, and let them try the experiment of free labor for themselves. They had earned it by the faithful labor of three generations; and their masters deserved such punishment for being found in armed rebellion against the United-States Government. But it is not always possible to do the best thing; and, in the present case, no such Spartan justice could be dealt to our white enemies and black friends. The enlistment of blacks had at that time almost entirely ceased. What caused the calm, I do not know. We were not equal to so grand a measure. We needed that the vast tide of death should roll by our own doors, and sweep away our fathers and sons, before we could come to our senses, and give the black the one boon he has been asking for so long, — permission to fight for our common country, and against his oppressors and our enemies.

There can, therefore, be no question in the mind of any thinking man, that it was far better to induce these negroes to return to their homes, and get in a crop for the coming season, than to allow

them to live on the Government rations, and do
nothing but contract vicious habits by reason of
proximity to our camps. These were the very
strong reasons that urged me to undertake the
work of putting the labor system into operation.

I did not wholly like the agreement between the
Government and the planters. I never believed in
the permission which was given to the latter to
raise a cane-crop. They did not deserve to have
their interests consulted in this matter. The
whole plan was devised and executed for the well-
being of the negro alone. So long as the planter
holds any legal rights in the slave, he will be the
enemy of the Government; and his rights, so called,
are not to be thought of for a single moment. I
regretted, therefore, that a spear of cane was
allowed to show itself above the ground. I would
have had nothing but a crop of corn and vegeta-
bles, — products which will not find their way into
the pockets of our foes, but into the stomachs of
our friends. Still this could not be urged, forsooth,
because our over-careful President was desirous to
conciliate. There had been harsh measures enough
in this department; and since Butler had stroked
the cat from tail to head, and found her full of
yawl and scratch, it was determined to stroke her
from head to tail, and see if she would not hide

her claws, and commence to purr. So the planter
was touched very tenderly, if he was touched at
all.

The labor system was well enough in its conception. The central idea was just and humane. It
required, however, to be carefully watched, lest
the overseers of plantations should get back to
their old tricks with the whip, and lest the planters
themselves should fail to give their hands proper
food and clothing. The plan would undoubtedly
work well, provided this vigilance was active; and
provided, again, that, in case of a flagrant misde-
meanor of this kind, the offender should be visited
with condign punishment, and the plantation
stripped of every thing, as a reminder that the
old times have gone by, and the new times have
come. In other words, it would be successful, if the
planters were made aware that the labor system
and slavery are two very different things, and not
synonymous.

The worth of the plan has been practically illus-
trated. The great majority of the negroes have
been rendered comparatively happy and contented.
They have homes. They do not work during the
hottest part of the day. They have their families
about them, and are higher in the social scale, and
more independent and more cheerful, than they
have ever been before. They know that they are

no longer chattels. They are very rapidly learning their own power and worth. In every contest between the master and his slaves, the latter invariably win the day. They have a mine of strategy, to which the planter sooner or later yields. For instance: A few days ago, a gentleman below the city hired a new overseer, one who was obnoxious to the hands on account of his reputation. He was in the habit of wielding the whip pretty freely, and of using abusive language to the negro women. On the morning when he arrived to enter on his duties, a delegation from the field-hands waited upon the proprietor, and very respectfully stated their objections against the new-comer. When they had finished, the master indulged in some very strong language, — forgetting that times had somewhat changed, — and bade them go about their business, telling them that he would hire whomsoever he chose to be overseer. They remonstrated still further, saying that the hands could not work under such a man, but that they would work cheerfully under any one else. He dismissed them with an oath. The matter, however, did not end there. The delegation at once went to their cabins, packed up their little bundles, and started on the road to Fort Jackson. They knew, that, once there, they could get employment. They had not gone far, however, before the master came to his senses.

He was no longer the owner of mere chattels.
Some change had come over slavery; and he was
surprised to find that those whom he had so often
stigmatized as " things," and counted at so much
" per head " as he did his cows and hogs, were
growing very rapidly into the likeness of men,
" who know their rights, and, knowing, dare maintain." He called them all back; told them they
should have any overseer they wanted: upon which
they unpacked their bundles, and went quietly to
the field, as if nothing had happened.

At Berwick's Bay there is no labor system, and
the negroes are in a most deplorable condition.
Six thousand came from the plantations between
the bay and Alexandria; and are living in such a
way, that the mortality during the summer will be
most terrible. The able-bodied men have enlisted.
The old, the young, and the women are living in
little huts, with nothing to do, with no comforts
when they are ill, and with more than a fair prospect of a speedy death before them. They are
free; but, alas! freedom only means the power to
die. Their proper place, indeed the only place
where they can learn the meaning and the privileges of freedom, is on the plantation, as hired
hands. Then, if one or two or a thousand are able
to do something better than dig corn, they ought to
have perfect liberty to try their pluck and their

luck in the city. In this way, there will be a home
to start from; a home where the wife and children
earn their daily bread, while the sturdy father is
working his way in the great world up to a dollar
a day. But this taking the negroes from the plantations where they can and should be protected,
and huddling them together where they must
starve and die, proves the worth of the labor system, when carried out in the right spirit.

I was very much gratified to have the general
superintendence of this experiment; for it gave me
an opportunity to visit all the plantations in the
department, and afforded me an insight into Southern life. I entered upon the work at once, and
with alacrity. I visited nearly every important
place from Baton Rouge to Fort Jackson. I saw
planters in their best and in their worst moods:
when they were glum; when they wanted to be
impudent, and, not quite daring to be so for fear of
consequences, set their wives on me, — from whose
tongues I invariably beat as hasty a retreat as possible; and when they were in good humor, and
ready to give me any data I desired.

Here the remembrance of my sufferings from
the climate of the lower part of the State comes
up so vividly, that I must be allowed to make a
digression in order to describe it. Of all things
horrible, most horrible, this is certainly the worst.

To say it is unhealthy, is to be very complimentary. The soil of the country is made up
of vegetable matter, which is yet in the process of
decomposition. Dig down three feet, and you
come to water. In twenty-four hours, that water
exhales a most nauseous odor, which no one can
take into his lungs with impunity. If you sleep
out of doors, no matter what precautions you may
take, you will be sure to succumb to an attack of
chills, which will rack your system, and make you
hollow-eyed and hollow-cheeked in a few days. If
you get sick with fever, the chances are that you
will not get well. Physicians tell me that medicines fail here which have never been known to
fail at the North. There is nothing vitalizing in
the air. A man comes to this country with his
vital mercury at eighty. In a little while, he
catches cold, and the mercury sinks to sixty.
Slowly, slowly, it moves upward; but it always
stops somewhere among the seventies. It will not
get up to the full eighty again; and, every time he
is ill, the less chance there is of his getting well.
There is no place on the river, south of Baton
Rouge, where one can live the exposed life of the
soldier with impunity. The most rugged systems
yield by degrees to the fatal miasm with which the
night air is laden; and boys, who in Maine, two
years ago, cut, split, and piled their two cords of

wood a day, go regularly at surgeon's call to get their five grains of quinine.

Indeed, none of the lower part of the State has yet reached that geological age in which the soil is fit for the residence of man. Had it been let alone for a couple of centuries, the many thousands of tons of sediment which the river daily brings from the North, and which it is now compelled to deposit at the passes, — every year thrusting the land out into the sea some two hundred feet, — would have been spread by the kindly hand of Nature over the whole area of Lower Louisiana, and the State would by this time have attained an average elevation of six feet above its present mosquito and alligator level.

The proper hint to civilizers was given by De Soto, who struck north-west from Mobile, and landed somewhere near the mouth of the Red River. But Cavalier de la Salle, in 1682, paddled up the river from its mouth; and when the Iroquois met in solemn conclave to determine whether permission should be given to the white man to settle, and their chief Mansoria had decided in the negative, he appeared in person before the grave council, and used such eloquent and persuasive words, that the voice of the chief was drowned, and the fatal permission obtained. It was indeed a *grave* privilege which the red man yielded to the

whites.   The vast chemical processes were inter-
fered with; and to-day, instead of having a territory finished by Nature, with her signature on it,
"It is good for the habitation of man," we have
a country in which man insists upon living, but
which is fit only as a home for the alligator and the
snake.

To a stranger, this language may seem extrava-
gant; but, to one who has lived in these parts, it is
exceedingly moderate.   Take a stroll some fine day
from the planter's house, along the road leading to
the woods.   The air is filled with a universal hum.
It is the singing of the mosquitoes, who come in
dense clouds, and sometimes in such countless
numbers, that even the mules, though covered from
ears to tail with bagging, refuse to work, and the
horses are literally sprinkled with blood.   But be
careful how you walk; for there lies across your
path that prototype of some Northern politicians,
the copperhead!   And be careful again; for I
hear the warning rattle of the only chivalrous
snake in the woods!   And, now that you have
reached the sluggish bayou, you notice at a glance
a dozen square-built, roof-like heads moving slowly
on the surface of the water.   These uncouth, un-
gainly creatures, who disport themselves regardless
of your presence, seem to be the representatives of
a distant geological period.

The overhanging woods, the tall, broad, live-oak, and the forlorn-looking, spire-like cypress, are covered with aerial moss, which clings to all the branches, and hangs gracefully down for six or eight feet. As you look at the picture, remembering the nature of the soil under your feet, and looking round on the tall, rank grass covering the prairie, you are surprised at your own presence in such a scene. It belongs, not to the present, but to the distant past.

It must not be forgotten, that I am now speaking of Lower Louisiana. The scenery from Baton Rouge northward is very fine. The ground is undulating, the air is pure, the reptiles and vermin are less numerous, and the country is more healthy; but our soldiers have been stationed on the lower coasts of the river, and have contracted all manner of diseases from the fatal climate.

I was gratified that my position gave me an opportunity to look into the social life of the South, and compare it with that of the North. I have always had an awe of what has been termed the " chivalry and high breeding of the South." I early fell into the popular ruts; and when A. H. Stephens said, as a matter of course, that the new Confederacy was to be made up of the *élite* of the world, I was ready to admit, that in open-handed generosity, and a certain social polish, the sun did

operate in different ways upon those south and
north of Mason and Dixon's line. But I had not
travelled far, before this matter and its philosophy
were made plain. I saw at once where all this
balderdash came from, and only laughed at myself
for my folly in being duped so long. There are, in
the South, a certain number of families who boast a
well-to-do ancestry. They are, in pecuniary matters, far above want. They are proud, as they
have a right to be, of their grandfathers ; and
they cultivate the fine arts, and bear themselves
with the dignity becoming a good position. This
society of exclusives is, however, small. It is
everywhere small. But the aristocratic institutions of the country make these few families the
apex of the historic and social cone, always prominent, and a sort of beacon-light by which all the
rest of society is governed. Now, in the North, we
have just as many families who are well-to-do in
the world, and whose grandfathers were very
respectable personages. They also cultivate the
fine arts, and are distinguished everywhere by
their gentlemanly bearing. They travel, visit the
worthiest celebrities of Europe, bring home a re-
fined polish of manner, and a certain ease, which
mark the gentleman everywhere. But these first
families are not necessarily prominent marks, when
you look at our social life ; because the whole struc-

ture of our society is democratic. They do not
openly lead society; for all about them is a hurry
and a bustle, in which their presence is wholly
forgotten. Ask a Louisianian who are the best
families of the State, and he will instantly put his
right fore-finger on his left fore-finger, and begin
with number one. Ask a man from the Bay State
the same question, and he will tell you he does not
know, and does not care. The two answers are
entirely characteristic.

This boast of ancestry is all very well in its way;
but when one's neck is constantly crooked over his
shoulder, and one's lips are ever recounting the
brave deeds of another, it suggests unpleasant
reflections concerning the imbecility of the present
representative of the family. If one can do nothing himself, it is well enough for him to spend
his time studying the biography of his ancestors.
And yet I confess to a sort of disagreeable feeling
as I enter a house pervaded with this musty atmosphere. It takes my breath away: and, as I look
up at the dingy old portrait of him in the big bag
wig, — the sturdy old root from which has grown
these many genealogical shoots, — I feel a certain
awkwardness; for it always seems to look down on
me with hard eyes, and as though it would say,
" Young man, *your* grandfather was nothing but an
honest Yorkshire mechanic; and, while he was ply-

ing his trade, I was on the high seas, the captain of an 'Alabama.'" And then the dingy old portrait seems to hang against the wall more stiffly than ever. However, I have never allowed these reflections to interfere with my duty; and I have never found among the grandchildren of these great ones any thing to remind me that they were more than common dust. It is certainly one of the pleasantest and most prophetic characteristics of the true republican, — and I claim the right to be known as such, — that he is taught never to stand in the shadow of his father's doings, but to step boldly out into the world, and grow to such manly proportions, that he also may cast a shadow forward upon the future. The real American never says, " My father did that : " he puts his hands on some fair achievement, and says, "*I* did that with my own brown hands and my own tough brain."

Now, leaving these few privileged ones who sit on the upper seat, I asked myself, Who are the planters of this State, who have thundered forth during the last fifty years their claim to be considered the true " American gentlemen " ? What right have they to raise this eternal din of boasting which assails our Northern ears ? What is there, in their ancestry or in themselves, that they should climb to the top of a pedestal of their own making, and clamor so boisterously of their better blood and breeding, that the masses of the North half admit their loud-mouthed claims, and the people of Europe believe, that, for refinement and all gentlemanly parts, they must look below the manufacturing States?

First, then, in the catalogue, come the Creole families. These are a class of people generally descended from the old French settlers; and, as they seldom speak English, they live in a circle by themselves. Some are wealthy, and very many are poor. The former are frequently very wealthy, and the latter miserably poor. They form a very exclusive clique, whose members intermarry, and thus keep in a certain round of families whatever property may be accumulated. I am not wrong in saying, that this Creole population is not generally regarded as forming any thing more than a part of the respectability of the body social. They are characterized by more than the usual cruelty to their servants; and are not noted for either polish of manner, or refinement. On looking over the slender library of one of these families, I found a splendidly bound and entire edition of Paul de Kock's novels. The rest of the library consisted of works of a light character, and seemed to be a fair criticism of the class of people under review. They exhibit very little taste, either in the outside decorations of their houses or in the

internal arrangements. They have lost that peculiar delicacy which is the charm of the real French
character, which decorates a room in such a way,
that, the moment you enter, you are impressed
with the feeling, that a cultivated person has been
there before you; and, in becoming Anglicized, are
satisfied with a bare wall, a plain bedstead and
bureau, and a general confusion and chaos, which
at once dispels all reverence for the present generation of the followers of Bienville and Iberville.

Once in a while, you find one who traces his
pedigree back to these daring adventurers, and
then you discover some attempt at refinement; but
most of the Creoles are simply descendants of the
rank and file of these leaders, who have crept up
to competency, and who show the nature of their
past by the coarseness of their present.

There is no doubt that I saw these families under
the most unfavorable circumstances. They were
generally registered enemies, who, by their manner,
showed plainly enough that they were aware of
their living simply by the suffrage of the United-
States Government. The men were sullen and
ugly. The women (even those who claimed to have
princely blood in their veins) sometimes forgot
their sex, and descended from the lofty position
of the lady to the common earth of the fish-woman.
They were vindictive, never losing an opportunity

to insult us; and one, whom we had occasion to
meet on the Têche, went so far as to malign us in
a note which she requested me to carry to the city.
The note was, of course, open when given to me;
but the lady wrote in French, presuming that a
poor mudsill could be easily duped. I placed it in
my pocket, never dreaming that one of the real
chivalry could do an uncourteous action. Before I
got back to the city, however, I thought it well to
know what I was doing in thus carrying a letter
from one living in a hostile land. I discovered
that my lady hostess had indulged in a nice little
French tirade against our forces, and prayed that
God would send us defeat; and the rebels, victory.
I was indignant that I had neglected to read the
note in the woman's presence; for I could then
have resented the insult. It was only left to me,
however, to pocket my chagrin, and to commit the
offending epistle, with all its beautifully written
anathemas against the good old flag, to the unhealthy waters of the nearest bayou.

The next class forms the bulk of Louisiana
planters. It is largely composed of men, who,
twenty years ago, left the North, and settled in the
South, for the simple and very laudable purpose of
making money. They came here poor; bought and
cleared a few acres of land; after years of toil,
and the constant energy and shrewdness which

mark the Northerner, absorbed into their original
few acres the little plots of the neighboring small
planters; and now sit down in the midst of their
thousand acres, — half or two-thirds of which are
tilled by from fifty to two hundred negroes, — and
talk about good society. That they have been successful, is a compliment to us. We as well as they
feel a sort of pride in the wealth of one who has gone
from us with a Northern education, and built up a
fortune by his own native vigor of character.   It
is well enough that Mr. Brown, twenty years ago,
took to New Orleans a stallion, which he traded
for a good round sum, and that he crept up from
his position as a jockey to that of a wealthy planter.
But when Mr. Brown, with a remarkable self-com-
placency, keeps half a dozen "niggers" running
about the house to bring him matches, tobacco,
pipe, and tells you with *hauteur* of the innate
superiority of the Southern character, and puffs
his tobacco-smoke to the ceiling as he dilates on
the pettiness of the Northern nature, it certainly
makes you feel that a groom is a good fellow in
his place, and that many a man, who can rub a
horse down till he looks smooth and sleek, finds
himself greatly embarrassed when he comes to
play the gentleman.

Now, the majority of planters in the State are
Eastern or Western men, emigrants. They are

sharp, brilliant in business, and compare favorably with the same class of people in New York or Massachusetts. But that they should lay claim to any thing more than respectability, is simply ludicrous. The fact is, there is no such thing as an aristocracy in Louisiana, except such as exists in every community, and is based on money. As in every other State in the Union, there is, as I have mentioned, a small clique who look upon their ancestry with pride; and a literary clique, composed of men who belong to the learned professions, — men who have made their mark as authors or statesmen; and a larger clique, composed of the land-owners, who have a firm footing on a large pile of money. If I have rightly classified the people of the State, and *ex uno disce omnes*, I am sure it will be seen that there is no ground for this grand din about the Southern gentleman. No falsehood is more palpable than this, which has been iterated and reiterated in the Southern church, in Southern literature, in every political speech, until at last, when the war broke out, it showed itself in the opprobrious epithets which were cast upon the Northern character. It has been a habit, for years, for them to give, and for us to receive, such insults: and yet, if you would find a man, who, for the sake of the money he can make, will resort to the very meanest of measures; will

buy poor bacon to feed his two hundred hands ;
withal, will keep them on short allowance, while he
gives extra pay to an overseer to see that their
backs are well scored if they do not work, — you
need not go to the money-loving North. The men of
New Orleans will gash their consciences as deeply
as will the men of New York. Up the river, down
the river, and far in the inland parishes, you will
find "honorable men," men of good family, who
would resent an insult to their personal honor with
sword or pistol, who yet are knowingly, wilfully,
and inhumanly cruel to their hands, in order to get
a large crop. They cheat the negroes out of their
food and out of their clothing. They use the whip
with infernal license, and all for dollars and cents ;
and, at the same time, sneer at your prudence and
mine, as evidence of stingy souls.

These very men, when you call on them as a
friend, will bring from the cupboard their rich
wines, and charm you by their conversation as
they tell you that their slaves do just as they have
a mind to, and that they are losing money on them
every year, but keep them because they love
them next to their own children. They are lying
to you all this while. They are lying systema-
tically ; and, if you will take the pains to go into
the slaves' cabins at night, you will find out how
much these men love their slaves, and how much

the slaves love their owners. I have heard all this
rhetoric of the planter; and, at first, I believed it.
I began to think slavery was really a patriarchal
institution ; that the owner was a kind of father to
all his people, — feeding them and clothing them,
and caring for them tenderly when they were ill.
But one day, after I had listened to a long chapter
of this kind, I was driving out of the gate, when I
was stopped by a mulatto girl, who held something
in her hand which she evidently wanted me to examine. I reined up the horse; when she put into
my hand a thick iron ring, which she had been
compelled to wear about her ankle until it had
made a festering sore. Three others, who knew
our mission, came up ; and one showed my friend
Wheelock his bare back, which was cut and gashed
by the lash that had been applied only two days
before; and I said, " A Southern gentleman, a man
who despises money, will, after all, lie ! "

I afterwards found this to be universally true.
You may talk with a planter upon almost any subject, and you will find him affable and gentlemanly.
He will scorn to misrepresent an event, and will
speak with commendable charity of his neighbors.
The moment, however, the conversation edges
towards slavery, his demeanor changes. He either
grows reticent, and refuses to say a word; or else
becomes angry, and openly insults you on the spot.

There is no such thing as a calm discussion of the subject with him : he seems to think that any assertion, true or false, is fair. If he can adduce facts, he will pile them up; until, at last, you begin to think the best thing the Almighty can do is to get up an extra generation of negroes for the use of the Southern sugar-planter. If the facts are not readily handled, he hammers away at the Old Testament; quoting verse after verse, trying to prove that that venerable book has no higher mission than to afford favorite texts for the slaveholder. If you suggest that the thraldom of a race impedes civilization, and is an inhumanity done to the enslaved, he harangues you on the value of the institution as a missionary society. It has elevated a whole people from the depths of barbarity to —

"The stocks, the lash, and the adulterous bed of the overseer, as the numerous mulattoes on every plantation will testify," I could not help saying one day, as I listened to one of these special pleaders.

"Not a slave has been whipped on this plantation for over two years," he replied in a tone of offended dignity. "The whip was abolished long ago. My slaves will all tell you they are happy and contented. I have told them over and over again, that, if they wish to leave the place, they can do so at any time. I beg you to examine this matter, and ascertain the truth of my assertion."

It was very ludicrous; but in my pocket I had a little memorandum, which ran thus: "Mr. Williams's plantation. Number of hands on place at present time, a hundred and fifty; number that ran away six months since, a hundred and forty-two. Complaints registered, that boy Tom and girl Mary were both inhumanly whipped last Thursday."

I do not mean to include in my severe criticism all the planters of the department. A few are really kind to their hands; and upon those plantations there has been no trouble, even in the midst of the chaos of the last eighteen months. Still there are but two plantations, south of New Orleans, on which there has not been more or less confusion.

I can say with all sincerity (and I have visited most of the plantations in the department of the Gulf), that, as a general thing, the planters do not live in as well-made or comfortable houses, do not arrange their grounds with as much taste, and do not exhibit as much intelligence, as that large class at the North which enjoys what is called a competency.

I do not believe, that in point of culture, or in actual enjoyment of life, the moderately wealthy class in the South will compare with the same class in the North. The only subject which they have made an especial study is politics. They follow the

course of their representatives in Congress far
more closely than we do, and take a sort of family
pride in saying kind things of them. They are our
superiors in a certain amount of ready but always
one-sided knowledge of national affairs; but, in
other paths of literature, they are sadly deficient.

This may be called an over-statement: and yet
every one who has travelled in the South will bear
me out in the assertion, that planters' houses, with
few exceptions, are poorly built, and without regard to taste; are ill-looking and meagre; that,
inside, there is very seldom any attempt at orna-
ment, — oftentimes nothing but bare walls and the
plainest furniture. It is often said, that this is very
natural among a people who live almost wholly out
of doors. I answer, So does the family that has a
summer-house in Swampscott or on Nantasket live
out of doors. Still you will find such a summer
residence arranged with great care and taste. The
furniture, the paintings, the library, — all indicate
taste and refinement on the part of the owner. The
Cuban lives out of doors, and his walls are never
decorated: his house is bare throughout. True;
and few, who know the Cuban, will claim for
him either good taste, refinement, or education.
No. The facts of which I speak denote a decided
weakness in the Southern planter's character. It
is the natural result of his lonely, insulated, un-

social life. There is nothing in his surroundings to make him feel the want of these things. His mind and tastes and heart inevitably fit themselves to his hermitage. It is one of the misfortunes of a planter's life.

Among other interesting subjects upon which I desired to get information was this vexatious question of free labor. I have always been startled by the assertion of those whose long experience entitled their opinion to respect, that forced labor was an absolute necessity in the South. To be sure, I have in my own mind believed the statement to be the result of bigotry or interest; and so I was only too glad to have an opportunity of looking into the matter for myself.

After a hard day's drive, I had been sitting, in the cool of the evening, in the gallery of a planter's house, chatting upon indifferent topics. At last, hoping to elicit some spark on this subject, I said, —

"What think you, sir, of free labor? Do you believe the negro can be hired to work, as are the laborers of the North?"

"No, sir," he replied: "free labor, as it is called, will inevitably prove a failure in the South. The negroes are naturally a low, lazy set. They are not influenced by any desire of gain, as are all the members of the white race. When they have

4

earned a dollar, they will do nothing until it is gone, and starvation compels them to work again. I have lived among them twenty years, and I know them to be a dependent race."

"And yet, sir, you told me, not long since, that your carpenter and blacksmith and groom and house-servant were all bright and intelligent; and your market-man also, who sells the greater part of your garden-produce. Surely these men are not dependent: they can earn their living anywhere and at any time. Now, why would it not be possible for you to hire these men as we do our laborers in the North; and, indeed, to hire all your other hands in the same way?"

"For this very obvious reason. Sugar is a crop not native to the soil of this State: it is what we term a forced crop. In Cuba, for instance, the sugar-planter takes no care of his grounds at all. When once his sugar-cane is planted, the rattoons will last from ten to fifteen years. Not so here. We are compelled to nurse our cane, to plough, to hoe, and to exercise constant vigilance; and in the fall, when the crop is almost ripe, we have all the way from twenty to a hundred thousand dollars at stake. We are afraid of the frosts. One cold night costs us thousands of dollars. We are compelled to commence grinding our cane before it is wholly ripe, in order to get through before the frosts take us. Now, in the grinding-season, we work our mills night and day. The season lasts generally three months. We must have absolute control over our hands during that time. If they refuse to work, we must have power to whip them. It is necessary to be able to reckon with perfect certainty on a given number of laborers; and unless we have this forced labor, which you call slavery, we shall have to give up the sugar-crop, and you people of the North will have to " —

" Give two cents a pound less for sugar than we do now," I could not help rejoining.

" What do you mean ? "

" Why, sir, what you, of course, already know. This State yields us about one-quarter of the sugar used in America. In order to protect this sugar interest, a tariff is required of all sugars imported from Cuba; and the result is, that the poor throughout the whole United States are compelled to give from one to two cents extra for every pound of sugar consumed, simply because you are determined to raise what your soil was never intended to raise. And, besides this mere monetary imposition, you insist that the institution of slavery, or forced labor, shall be ceded, in order that you may make your crops profitable."

He at once met me by throwing square in my face a long text from Moses; and I saw that the

conversation was at an end. I can stand bolt upright, and take a man's facts; indeed, they are what
I seek: but I confess to perfect powerlessness,
when, after detailing to him a long catalogue of
statistics which to me are perfectly conclusive, he
quietly gets up, and, bringing out the old family
Bible, turns to the dog-eared parts of the Pentateuch which he has pondered over so often, and
hurls at me his " THUS SAITH THE LORD." There is
no chance for argument then. You may be well
assured that your antagonist is working on a piece
of deep strategy; and it is best for you to start at
once for the other side of the Rappahannock.

Now, I am not at all inclined to deny this gentleman's facts. There is no doubt whatever that the
sugar-crop of the South is a forced crop. The cane
in Cuba grows with wonderful vigor, and spreads
over the surface of the ground until it has become
a perfect network. In the South, on the contrary,
it is planted in rows four or six feet apart; and the
rattoons never spread, and last only three years at
most. It may be true, too, that forced labor is an
absolute necessity to secure the crop in the autumn.
It certainly is not to be doubted, that the Southern
crop is protected by a tariff, because it costs the
planters two cents a pound more to raise the crop
than it does the Cuban. But, in view of these facts,
I most respectfully submit, that it would be good

policy on the part of the United States to buy up the landed property of Louisiana, and sell it again to the ten thousand little Creole-planters who have been by degrees crowded out of their farms by the large land-owners, on condition that not a stalk of cane shall ever be allowed to come out of the ground. If we can't have sugar without the stain of slavery, then let us go without it. The poor man of Ohio and Kansas ought not to be compelled to pay an extra price for one of the most necessary of his domestic wants, because thirteen hundred land-owners persist in raising a given crop in spite of the prohibition of Nature.

The next evening, I had the pleasure of stopping with a frank, open-hearted gentleman, who gave me the other side of the free-labor question. He believed in slavery, and was equally pugnacious upon the subject with my friend of the night before; but putting the black man out of sight entirely, and speaking of the expense of conducting a plantation, he opened up one or two facts which I regarded as important, and which I afterward fully corroborated. He owned some two hundred and fifty people. Of these, not more than sixty, or seventy-five at most, could be reckoned as good, able-bodied field-hands. The remaining two-thirds were old, young, decrepit, or in the hospital. There were between thirty and forty children on the place. As a general rule, not more than one-third of the people on the older plantations are fit for service. This is a fair average, as I proved by my later experience. Now, these people are all to be supported. They all draw their rations of food and clothing ; and though these are both poor enough, yet, in the aggregate, the expense must be considerable. So I said to my friend, —

" Would it not be cheaper for you to hire these sixty or seventy hands, who carry on your place, at good wages, than to own them, with all the risks of disease and death, and be compelled to support this long train of dependants ? "

" Most assuredly," he replied at once. " If it could be so arranged, I would willingly give every able-bodied hand on the place a dollar a day, the year through. Slaves are costing more every year. The price of good, able-bodied hands has more than doubled in the last twelve years. Free labor can no doubt be made a success. Still, slavery is one of the rights of the South ; and is, of a truth, the salvation of the African race."

Here followed the same stale arguments which I had been through with a dozen times. At last, however, he got excited, and referred to the West Indies as proof that the only proper condition of the negro is one of dependence.

" Were you ever in Jamaica ? " I asked, turning the conversation to matters of travel.

" Yes, sir. I spent some three months in Jamaica."

" Who were the custom-officers there, sir ? "

" Men as black as your hat. It surprised me when one came upon deck, and, in a very gentlemanly way, asked to see our trunks ; and when the preliminaries were through, and the captain asked him into the cabin, he gave us as neat a little speech as I ever heard, and, in all respects, bore himself like a gentleman."

" And yet this man, also, is one of the dependants. You were not ashamed to be seen drinking with him, and you listened to his speech with pleasure ? "

He afterward spoke of going into society, and meeting the blacks familiarly, — lawyers, judges, military officers, and scholars ; and did not express any repugnance at such intimacy.

Nothing surprised me more than this tame, trite assertion concerning the natural dependence of the negro, and his unfitness to get his own living. Not only does every plantation in the State contradict the statement, but also a large class of free persons of color in every city, who not only support their families, but by their shrewdness have succeeded in laying up quite a little fortune against a time of want. When I went through the Têche country, I visited very many farms, from those of a few acres to those which spread over an area as large as most plantations, which were owned and carried on by free persons of color. These people exist in sufficient numbers to form a class, and, though tabooed from all good white society, live quite happily, and in the enjoyment of fortunes ranging all the way from thousands to hundreds of thousands of dollars. They are known as a quiet, thrifty community. They have no rights, of course, under the State laws; but their well-conducted plantations amply prove, that the ability to take care of one's self exists independently of any color of the skin. With such examples as these scattered through the country, a shrewd, wealthy black, alternating with a white man, whose vacant stare and squalid poverty stamp him at once as a member in good standing of that large community composed of poor trash, it is worse than puerile for a planter to assert concerning the one race, that it is by nature dominant; and of the other, that it was intended by the Almighty to do the white man's bidding. The free negro who makes his hundred or two hundred bales of cotton every year, is, by all the laws of God and man, a part of our civilization, entitled to all the rights and privileges of citizenship; and the State that, by law or

public opinion, deprives him of one iota of such
rights, is recreant to its trust, and unworthy a
place in to-day's history. He is one of the real
aristocrats; and all your laws, and all your scoffs
and taunts and miscalled facts, will fail to reduce
him to the ranks. And the poor devil of a white
man, who sits in the doorway sucking his dirty
fingers, with no ambition, a mere lump of animated
putty, with a brain as solid and useless as so much
wet clay, is a base plebeian; one intended to serve;
a man who cannot take care of himself : and you
may legislate until doomsday ; you may decree
him a member of the dominant race as much as
you please, — it is of no use. There is no fire in
him, no life, no soul. He crawls : he does not
stand erect. So this question of dominance is not
one of race, but of individuals. There are some
born to rule, but they are not all white. There
are many born to serve ; but they are not all black.
To serve or rule is a right which is not written in
the skin, but in the head.

These two evenings threw a vast deal of light on
this subject of free labor. That it may be made a
success, there is no longer any doubt. Indeed, it
has been proved, that a profitable crop of sugar
can be raised by white labor, although far more
expensive than black labor. But the plan is an
innovation, and will meet with great opposition

from many of the planters, — men who do not belong to the South, but who came here for the simple purpose of speculation.

There is one class of men only who readily concede that it may be made a success. It consists of those who have lived here forty and fifty years; who have a large number of unproductive hands, old and young, — people who have grown up on the plantation, and who are part and parcel of it. The owners do not like to sell them: indeed, they are not worth any thing. Still, they amount to a great deal, when the expenses of the place are reckoned. There is another class, generally consisting of Northern men, who came here twenty years ago, determined on making money. These do not have the usual surplus of children and old people. Their hands are all able to work, and are mostly men. They, at first, buy the requisite number of "head" to carry on their place, assuring themselves that they are sound in wind and limb; and then, with an acuteness which is worthy of a better cause, they watch them day by day. When one falls sick, he is sold, and a stout hand substituted. Any exhibition of weakness is sufficient to bring one to the auction-block. In this way, the hands are always able-bodied; and there is no drag on the planter, of bills for the hospital, and other little inconveniences, which are experi-

enced on most plantations. This man is furious
when you talk to him of free labor. He speaks in
unmeasured terms of the abolitionists, and believes
that the President's proclamation has actually
ruined the country.

Still, there is no need of trembling in the presence of these men : there is more thunder than
lightning in them. Since their souls are so absorbed in dollars and cents, it only becomes necessary to inaugurate the system of free labor ; and
at the end of the first season, when the ledger,
which is their only Bible, gives its verdict in favor
of right and humanity, true to their instincts, these
financial weather-cocks will turn to free labor, and
support it so zealously, that you will almost be persuaded they are Christians. It is of no use to
argue with such men. They are more than ada-
mant to all your logic. But show them, at the end
of the year, the five-dollar bill on the right side of
the account, and they jump at it as quickly as the
early spring trout at the fly.

All the sacred texts of the Pentateuch will then
be forsaken. No more dog-ears, no more fumbling for new proofs. The converted men will sit
quietly in their pews when the minister speaks of
the equality of all men in the sight of God ; not a
scowl in their faces, not a hair on their heads
ruffled. It is, after all, the five-dollar bill that

supports the institution, and gives its authenticity
to the Old Testament. Slip the bill away, and
put it under the corner of the Temple of Freedom,
and how quickly all her aisles will be filled with
devotees! The millennium will commence at once.
Who can measure the length, breadth, or power of
a poor five-dollar bill?

I hope my friends will not judge, from this long
array of sharp criticism, that I am naturally of
an ill temper; that my liver was affected by the
miasm of the swamps; or that, in the hopeless
endeavor to brush away the clouds of mosquitoes,
who did very little cooing, but an immense amount
of billing, I saw things through the anathemas
and immense expletives which I showered upon
those musical insects. I am naturally of a very
mild temper, and do not fail to remember many
albœ dies spent among friendly planters and on
pleasant excursions. When I generalize, it is my
business to forget every thing, — the kind attentions gracefully offered to a weary traveller, the fair
hand proffering the refreshing wine, the soft bed
after the hard day's work, and the broiled chicken
of the next morning, — and see only a system, an
institution, in its many bearings on society; a
principle of political economy in all its practical
workings.

I have read a great many books of travel in the

South; and, I think, have generally discovered how they were written, and at what time of the day. Here is one, for instance, a queer little thing, with scarce a word of truth between the covers, praising all Southern society, and even daring to laud slavery. Now, though the thing is a literary curiosity, from the fact that it is false from beginning to end, you and I, who have been through the mill, can guess very well when all that honest rhetoric was written. I will tell you my guess; but you must not let it go farther. It is one of those things the public must not know. *It was just after dinner : it is a post-prandial production ;* a quiet little clerical joke, which the public does not understand.

Listen to my conjecture in detail. The future author was met at the station by a fine, talkative old gentleman, who at once made him feel, after his hard day's ride, that he had at last reached a haven of rest, where he might consider himself an honored guest. The racket of the cars was changed for the soft cushions of a carriage. His tired nerves were deliciously titillated by the pleasant garrulity of the old gentleman, who mingled fact, fiction, and witticism in his conversation. The house was reached. It was pleasantly surrounded by exquisitely fragrant orange-trees, whose fresh blossoms filled the air with perfume ; and, after a quiet cup of tea, the considerate host showed his weary guest to the chamber. Here, too, were flowers..

How full of good feeling and of refinement these Southern people are ! What distinguished manners ! — the lofty bearing of a prince, and yet the utmost suavity and geniality. What a difference between brick walls, hot and musty, and this ambrosial air, laden with the fragrance of wild roses and geraniums !

Just then, when the poor guest was half disrobed, a timid knock was heard.

" Come in ! "

The door opened, and a curly-headed, pretty little boy entered, — he is one of the flowers of rhetoric belonging to the system, — bearing a little waiter, with a pitcher of iced lemonade, with just enough claret in it to make it nectar.

" Massa sends dis, sir," said the bashful little fellow.

How kind, how considerate ! How remarkable these Southern people are for the delicacy of their attentions ! When the boy left the room, a thought entered the guest's head. He went to the South not merely for his health, but to see the institution ; and here was a piece of it trotting about the house, and bringing him ice-water. This chance was not to be lost. Opening the door, he cried, —

" Come back, my child : I want to speak to you."

The little fellow, who had never been addressed in that way before, hesitated a moment, wondering if he was the one meant; and then entered the room again.

" My little boy," said the guest, beginning his experience, and gently pinching the little slave's fat cheeks, " are you happy ? "

" Yes, massa," the child said, of course. There was nothing else to say.

" Does your master treat you well ? and do you have good things to eat, and a nice bed to lie on ? "

" Yes, massa."

Then the boy was dismissed, and the first impression of slavery was received. If I had only been at his elbow, I would have asked another question : —

" Boy, where's your father ? "

" Don'o, sir," he would have answered.

" Don't know, eh ? Haven't you ever seen him, or ever heard your mother talk about him ? "

" No, massa," he would have replied wonderingly. Now, look at his skin : it is a very delicate olive. *That boy never had any father !*

You see I have got my first impression of the institution. I got no iced lemonade, with claret in it; but I think I got hold of a very ugly fact instead.

The next day, just before dinner, the saddle-horses were at the door; and the guest trembled a little, no doubt, for he is not accustomed to the exercise: but there is no fear; for the beast is a blood-horse, and as gentle as a kitten. The rider has nothing to do but to keep still, and the well-trained animal lopes along most elegantly. Let us keep up with the old gentleman and the future author. Here are the fields: they stretch along two miles on the road, and are half or three-quarters of a mile deep. Behind them are the cypress-woods, extending indefinitely, sometimes six miles back to the lake. The affable old gentleman is an immense landed proprietor, fit to be a lord, and entirely unlike the small farmers of the North. At length, they reach the field where the hands are at work, — fifty, seventy-five, a hundred of them, — the men with nothing but pantaloons on, their backs shining in the sun; the women *à la Bloomer*, their skirts tucked above their knees, and on their heads sometimes a piece of a bonnet, again a straw-hat, and still again a red and yellow bandanna.

"There," says the host jocularly, "is the institution. Now, sir, those boys and girls were all raised on this estate. I took care of most of them when they were curly-headed tots. A great many of them can read and write. Some have money in the bank. They have their little chapel, where they praise God every sabbath. Sir, much as your Northern people say against us, we yet hold our slaves in deep regard. We are all one family. What I have, they have. They have plenty of food, and a good house. They are the most jovial set in the world; and could not, I verily believe, be hired to leave the estate. This, sir, is slavery: abolish it, and you throw these, my family, upon the cold charities of the world."

Now, that is certainly a very pretty thing to say. The guest believes every word of it. Why not? Will an affable old gentleman, who sends up to his chamber iced lemonade with claret in it, lie? The thought is unworthy.

Our Northern fanatics have vilified the institution. These people are in far better condition than the poor whites of New England. They are always properly cared for. Has not the host said it? Ah me! if only the wild abolitionists could sit on this saddle, and view this truly patriarchal scene, they would at once vote the Democratic ticket.

These are not exactly the words the guest's thoughts would assume, if he chose to utter them; but only my interpretation of what was going on in his mind.

By the way, the future author did not notice the
black boy, who all the while was standing close by
his horse, and who heard every word of the above
well-delivered speech; and consequently he lost
the queer expression of the fellow's face whenever the old gentleman became pathetic.

You've seen those bank-bills, which, for fear of
being counterfeited, are printed nearly all over
with one dollar, one dollar, one dollar? Well,
the boy's face was covered all over in the same
way with characters which any one could read;
and they were not quite complimentary to the affable old gentleman: so I shall not mention them
here. Nor did the author notice the sharp voice
of command with which the boy was ordered to
the field: so he got his second impression. I did
notice those two queer little incidents, and got my
second impression; and, if I should compare notes
with the guest, he would be greatly surprised at
the discrepancy in our opinions.

He forgot, too, to go to the cabins after dark,
and talk with the people, just to corroborate what
the old gentleman said about his love for hands;
and so didn't get any third impression at all. I
did do that thing, and was surprised to find one of
" the family " just from the whipping-house, with
his back all cut up, — a raw mass of flesh, made by
a long raw-hide lash; and there I found my third
impression.

After a while, the guest's book was written.
You and I know where to find the iced lemonade
in page one, the blood saddle-horse in page two,
and the affable and garrulous old gentleman in all
the rest of the book.   Still, these things are to be
kept from the public, who are to be left to wonder
how it is possible for Mr. A. to go South in May,
and Mr. B. to go South in June, and, going over the
same ground, to write books, — the one saying that
slavery is from heaven, the other that it is from
hell.   You and I know that it is simply because
they don't see the same things.   The one man sees
the planter, and the other man sees the plantation.

If, then, my book is full of sharp criticism, and
if I say more unpleasant things than pleasant ones
of the South, I pray you not to attribute it to my
temper so much as to my honesty.   Shall I say kind
things of an institution that is hateful, because
some of those who uphold it treat me with generous courtesy ?   Because my host comes in to say
" Good-night!" and wishes me pleasant dreams, shall
I borrow his spectacles, and swear that a thing is
sound, when my own eyes tell me it is rotten?   If
my host demands this, he is my enemy.   I must
look into every corner, and tell what I see.   I beg
you, therefore, to believe, that it was not the
absence of iced lemonade, with claret in it, which

is the motor to my severe language. I certainly
met with some pleasant gentlemen, and, through
their courtesy, enjoyed many a day of rare sport,
and visited many scenes which I recall with peculiar pleasure. Let me tell you of some of these
experiences.

Being very much worn with constant travelling
for weeks, Mr. Lawrence, of the Magnolia Plantation, about forty-five miles below the city, asked
Mr. Wheelock and myself to spend a few days with
him; and we at once cheerfully accepted his kind
invitation. We found him a very genial, hospita-
ble gentleman, and enjoyed our stay exceedingly.
We rode over his fine, large plantation; and hap-
pening to hit a half-acre of luscious, ripe black-
berries (it was in May), found ourselves in the
midst of the brambles in a surprisingly short time;
leaving the place with great hesitation, and then
only on condition that we should make daily visits
to the spot, or that the darkies should bring the
well-laden baskets to us. Day after day, we sat in
the gallery, enjoying the luxury of physical repose,
which seemed like a delightful, prolonged siesta.
A few quaint, old-fashioned books supplied us with
reading; and good-tempered but sometimes warm
discussions upon the topics of the day came in to
fill up the little interstices of time, when we otherwise might have felt the symptoms of ennui.

One day, our host told us that a few miles away were three of those mysterious mounds which the Indians left as a memento and a puzzle to the white man, and that we could go a part of the way through some of the finest scenery in the State. It was at once determined that we ought to make the trip: so the orders were given to have a skiff in the canal early in the morning, with Sam and Jim to handle the white-oak. A bright, beautiful morning it was. Soon after breakfast, the buggy drove to the door; and we rode to the canal, at the wood-end of the plantation, where we found our two sable friends ready. A half-mile through the canal, where we scared up an alligator ten feet long, who made the water foam when he went down, and we struck into the beautiful Chenière, a bayou about seventy-five feet wide, and one of that tangled web of bayous which drain the lower part of the State. We moved smoothly and quietly along, the silence broken only by the regular dip of the oars; all about us, on either side, an almost boundless prairie, level as a floor, and covered with tall, rank grass five or six feet high. I could not control my destructive tendencies, and landed twice to set it on fire; but succeeded only in making a huge smoke, which floated upwards in heavy black clouds, adding to the picturesqueness of the scene.

We went on in this way for a little while, when
the Chenière flowed through some woods which
gave us scenery wholly different.   On the banks,
and out of the rich marshy land, grew those wonderful live-oaks, uncouth but grand, which one
must see to appreciate.   So tough is the fibre, that
branches sometimes grow horizontally to incredible
lengths.   I remember seeing one branch thus
growing, which I measured, and found, to my surprise, that it was eighty feet long ; extending
almost at right angles from the trunk.   These long
branches stretch out over the water, forming the
most delightful shade ; while from them hangs, in
thick, rich folds, six feet long or more, this aerial-
moss, which makes every forest of the South so
picturesque.   It gives the tree the air of antiquity ;
and the knotty, rough, irregular character of the
live-oak strengthens the impression.   I thought, at
the time, that it was the most romantic, unreal,
weird, and yet fascinating picture I had ever
looked on.   But the illusion that it was the home
of the fairies was soon dispelled by the numerous
alligators, which were lazily lying on logs, or, ogre-
like, floating leisurely along, only their thin, long
heads visible.   They disappeared only when our
boat showed a desire on our part to cultivate too
close an intimacy.

At last, we reached the place where we were to

land, and take guides through the woods to the
hieroglyphics of ancient history. Two little huts
showed themselves just on the edge of the woods;
and farther on, in a cleared space, another, in
which lived, not the lowest of the " poor white
trash," but people deplorably dirty and incredi-
bly ignorant. The master of the first hut, who
was to be our guide, had reclaimed from the
swamp and forest a few acres of land, and had, at
his leisure and at sundry times, planted a few
orange-trees thereon, from which he hoped, in the
course of a few years, to enjoy a snug little income. How he managed to support himself in the
interim, I could not discover. There was no evidence of farming utensils having been used; for
thick clusters of weeds, of most luxuriant growth,
tangled our feet at every step. A little patch of
half an acre was planted with sweet potatoes.
That was the entire farm. The Creole fished and
hunted, and in that way supplied his table. When
he was successful, his dinner consisted of sweet
potatoes, plus a catfish or a piece of venison; and,
when he came home empty-handed, it consisted
simply of the aforementioned esculent. His neighbors enjoyed the luxury of a log-hut, the wide
cracks in which were not even plastered with mud.
Three men and a woman lived in it. I saw one
rude mattress, and was convinced that these simple

people lived in a perfectly natural way; and were, perhaps, being far from the contaminations of the city, delighting in a little golden age of their own.

However, be this as it may, we started for the mounds. It was a rude path we travelled, through acres of straight, slender cane-stalks, which would have excited me beyond measure in my Izaak Walton days; over fallen timber, and narrow bridges made of uncertain limbs; spanning black, slimy-looking, stagnant water; through clouds of every kind of pestiferous insect known to the naturalist. Such heat never was felt before. We reached the mounds in a very melting mood; and, clambering forty feet to the top of one, were compelled to build a smudge, and put our heads in the hot, wavy smoke, in order to be comfortable. What expedients will not a man resort to in pursuit of comfort!

We were, however, well repaid for our journey; for these great heaps of earth, burial-places, landmarks of history, or whatever they may be, — dumb mementos of the past, — were very interesting. They were like those cairns found in the West, in Labrador, and all along the Gulf-coast. Some have been opened; but nothing satisfactory has been discovered. A few huge boxes, some pieces of pottery, and a few rude agricultural or domestic utensils, are all that have ever been dug up. Whether they were made by the Indians, whom we have driven away; or whether they are as old as the Pyramids, relics of a race living here when the earth was young, in some dim, ante-historic period, — has not yet been decided.

We walked back to the guide's house; and while sitting on the steps, in the shade, found that he had been one of the brave defenders of Fort Jackson.

" Why did you go to the war? "

" Couldn't help it."

" Why not? "

" New-Orleans people came down, and took all the men off every little place."

" What were you fighting for? Do you know? "

" Yes, sir (very emphatically). 'Cause the rich planters got into a row about their damned niggers; that's all. They staid at home, got up a big excitement, and made all the poor men stop the bullets."

We rowed back again, more charmed than ever with the beautiful Chenière, where the vessels of La Fitte used to anchor, snugly ensconced and out of sight while he was laying in provisions for a long voyage. We had enjoyed a most delightful day; reaching Mr. Lawrence's at about five o'clock, where we found a dinner to which we did ample justice.

6

And now back to my position of critic.

The great passion of the Southerner is to become the owner of a large landed estate: his ambition is for broad acres and heavy crops. Out of these he makes his aristocracy, not based on learning nor personal worth nor ancestry, but on personal influence. The inevitable tendency is to centralize the power of the State, and to create a class of men who every year stand in bolder opposition to the levelling democracy of the North, and in greater antagonism to the principles of republicanism. It is they, not we, who have departed from the grand historic thought which lies at the centre of American civilization. Whatever may have been the immediate occasion of the war, it is plain that the cause of it was in the widely differing ambition of the two peoples. Driven by the force of our newspapers, our pulpits, our literature, our lyceums, and our schools, we are tending more and more directly to the extreme of democracy ; while they have always had an itching palm for the privileges of the English landed gentry, whom they have aped for half a century. They disgusted even a real Britisher, Mr. Russell, by their whinings after a prince. They are weary of republicanism, forsooth, because some poor fellow may stand between the wind and their nobility.

And they are ever pestering one with the power

of cotton. Go where you will, your ears are eternally dinned with sugar and cotton. You may commence a conversation on eclipses, and persist in your endeavors to steer clear of the fatal subject: you will sail along smoothly for a while; but the cry will soon come from the look-out, "Breakers ahead!" and, before you know it, you have run your vessel high and dry into a cotton or cane field. I have often suggested that there were in the market other staple products. I have ventured to mention the hay-crop and the corn-crop of the North; and once I grew warm, and entered into a dissertation, on the historic and politic economical value of the North. I spoke of the individualism which marks us, of our general thrift, our educated masses; and called the gentleman's attention to the fact, that the saw which cut the boards of his house was made in the North; that the nails he used daily, his ploughs, his carpets, his furniture, his beds, his knives and forks, his carriage, his clock, all came from the North. "These things," I said, "indicate that the people are intelligent, thoughtful, and worthy the place they occupy in the world's history as the exponents of a new political truth."

"Still you can't get along without cotton," was the only answer I could elicit. There is one writer in De Bow's Review who puts this material in its proper place. "There was a time," he says, "when, the number of slaves in the States being very small, an universal desire to emancipate manifested itself. It was a calamity to be dreaded above all things. But just at this juncture, just in the nick of time, and only ten years after King George had relinquished his rule in America, in steps King Cotton, forbidding by his power what the other had forbidden by his veto; viz., the abolition of slavery: and so *the negroes were saved.*"

This chivalrous king has done still more for the negroes. "It has fed them, clothed them, sheltered them, *protected them from the uncompromising civilization about them,* taught thousands of them to read and write, and converted thousands more to the Christian religion."

Think of this, ye careless abolitionists of the North! While you have been talking about fancied rights and wrongs, the generous slaveholder has completely, and, what is better, practically, solved the whole problem. Out of pure love of the tropic race, he has filled his fields with cotton-seed in the spring, sent his hands to school all summer, and reaped a crop of five hundred bales in the autumn. Your philanthropy has all failed; and the growth of cotton has proved that the slave should be a slave for ever, and fill the white man's pocket with gold.

"But, if you would learn the immense importance of this weed as a political and civil influence, you have but to imagine its temporary loss, and the awful consequences which must inevitably follow. It would close the mills of Manchester, and an eighth part of the population of England would, at a blow, be deprived of their means of support; trade and commerce would be completely paralyzed; and so intimately connected are the interests of the civilized world now, that this shock to the welfare of England and America would make the whole civilized world bankrupt. It would carry ruin to the abodes of people in Berlin, who have never seen a negro nor raw cotton, and imagine themselves uninterested in either. *It would shake, if not destroy, the throne of Louis Napoleon.*"

I have met all degrees of conceit, — the poor dandy, who flattered himself that his fine looks led captive every girl whom he met; the millionnaire, who proudly believed, that, with a nod of his head, he could produce an earthquake: but this reaches the sublime. It towers so high, that we forget to laugh, and only look to wonder.

It is very curious to look at such an assertion, made in 1860, in the light of the events of the last three years. A disaster has happened to the cotton-crop; and instead of being sold to fill the mills of Manchester, and hold up the throne of Napoleon, it has been used to keep shot and shell from our gunboats, and for breastworks by both rebel and Union forces. Still, the convulsion has not come. The " whole civilized world," instead of being bankrupt, is making money as fast as ever, and setting its wits at work to find a substitute for that, which, with its attendant evils, has brought on one of the bloodiest wars of history.

The Southerner does not seem to have any pride in the progress of ideas : he confines himself to his own State ; and, with a bigotry and want of logic which augur ill for his future, he clings with blind tenacity to State-rights, and persistently ignores the fact of a central government. Patrick Henry said, " I am not a Virginian; I am an American:" but the Southerner says, with equal fire, " I am not an American, but a Louisianian." The war must go on until it removes all obstacles, and we stand on some platform where we can have a community of feeling.

Hence it is, that what may be called the civilization of the South does not equal that of the North. You find there the old feudal times, with very little change to fit the new century. After you leave the large cities, you seem to enter into a new century, and to breathe the air, and see the sights, which belonged to France and England four hundred years ago.

The plantation is the old feudal estate. There is no moated wall, no draw-bridge, no row of stalwart men in armor clad to meet you at the entrance, and announce your arrival; but, in many essential points, the resemblance is complete. Here, in the castle, are those who hold undisputed authority over from one to three hundred human beings. They live a strange, aimless life. Time hangs on their hands heavily, and each day is but a facsimile of every other day in the year. Yonder, in those little sheds, are the followers, the serfs, the slaves, of the chief. They are purposely kept in ignorance, because learning would open their eyes to their degraded condition, and they would break their chains. Like the serfs of Russia, these people belong to the soil, and are sold with it. They are fed on the meanest food; live in the midst of all manner of uncleanness; are subject to the will and wishes of owner and overseer, who can score their backs until they are covered with mountain-ridges of calloused flesh; and the law of the State protects the master, and passes sentence of death on the sufferer if he shows the spirit of a man, and lifts his arm in his own defence.

There is an infinite gloom hanging over such a life. It may do for the brutal land-owner or baron of the fifteenth century; but it is a sorry picture with which to illustrate the pages of American history.

The President "builded better than he knew," when he struck a blow at this institution; and the people of our land should demand that he take back the words which exempt certain parishes, and make a clean sweep from one end of the country to the other.

It may be asked, seeing all this evil, have you not discovered, here and there, a spark of gold? My only answer is, that, after the most careful examination, I can see in the system only unmitigated evil for both planter and negro. No human nature can endure the life of the planter, and retain its integrity. Its inevitable tendency is to demoralize. This, every one, who has had opportunity for observation, will admit. That the laws of morality are very loosely kept, is abundantly evident from the large number of mulattoes to be seen everywhere; and it does not increase one's respect for the moral tone of society, when it is known that these things are regarded as a matter of course, even by the planters' families. When the ladies of her court attempted to tease Marie Antoinette about the *penchant* which Louis had for certain fair women, she replied, "Oh! we must certainly allow him some luxuries." Still, the state of society in the time of Louis is not one to be made a pattern for us. Mr. Russell, when dining with the Southern commissioners, says the celebrated Keyes affair was discussed, and the hot Southerners spoke of the summary way in which such things are treated by them. He adds, " An argument which can scarcely be alluded to was used by them to show that these offences in slave States had not the excuse which might be adduced to diminish their gravity, when they occurred in States where all the population were white."

Nothing is so saddening, to one who loves the whole of America, as this general want of any national pride, which oppresses one on every side in the South. I have ridden over hundreds of miles of Louisiana; have met with all classes of men, high and low, rich and poor: but nowhere did I find any who spoke of our country. There is no patriotism, in its large sense, in the Southern States. Since Calhoun became the representative and idol of the agricultural interests, and disseminated that political poison which produces such hallucination, that the Carolinian and Louisianian believe, that, when America is mentioned, their own particular State is meant, there has been no comprehensive patriotism in any of the slave States. I said to one, who was vehemently declaiming about sovereign States, —

" But, my dear sir, are the United States a myth? Is there no central Government, to which is intrusted a supervision over the whole ? Did

7

we buy this State of yours simply because we had
an overplus of money which we did not know how
to invest? Or, on the other hand, did Louisiana
become a component part of the indivisible integer
known as the United States, to be governed in all
local matters by her own citizens, and in all national concerns by the will of a majority of the
whole people?"

My ire was of no use. He had but one kind of
pride, — in his State. Material to the last degree,
he insisted on the final triumph of the Confederacy,
because cotton and sugar are necessary to the
world. Not a word about the right or wrong of
secession. These are arguments which pass for
just nothing in the Southern mind. It was all
arithmetic. England consumes so much cotton
annually. She has so many bales on hand. In so
many weeks, her mills will stop running. Then
her people will begin to clamor for bread. As a
natural consequence, intervention will come. The
Confederacy will be acknowledged, the blockade
will be raised, and the thing is done.

Perhaps!

Never in my life have I felt so much pride in
New England as since I have been among the
planters of this State. Never before did I believe
she exercised such influence. She is hated with a
hatred deep and bitter, because of her public

schools, and her most persistent notions of popular education; for her free press, which, with a
galling independence, discusses the merits of all
questions of national policy; for her pulpits,
whence come doctrines which keep the minds of
the people alive with quickening thought; and for
her large-hearted and continent-embracing patriotism, which denounces that selfish love of State
which forgets the whole country, and is absorbed
in the petty interests of the plantation. No wonder we are looked upon as the incendiaries of
America. But, if there were no hay-stacks nor
powder-magazines in the South, why should they
fear this open, free discussion? They can talk of
us as they please, and we will not mob their speak-
ers. They may criticise our institutions as bitterly
as they choose. We are not afraid when they
handle fire. They fear and hate us, only because
we are republican, and they are not. They hate
us for the same reason that aristocrats, or those
who would be such, hate true democrats the world
over, — because we are determined to enlarge the
boundaries of popular rights, and because our
pulpits and our press will thunder against
every thing which is anti-republican, wherever
it is found. Here is the chief source of trouble. The State flag is first; the national flag is
nowhere.

Believe me, there is but one remedy. It is to conquer these people by an irresistible force; persist in the war at all hazards and costs, until the victory is complete; enforce all national measures with a hand of iron; decree that every man who treads the soil shall be free, and that wealth and position and fame are open to competition by all; and then leave half our army to settle in the lands they have conquered. Then will the radical change come.

Sure am I, that not till then shall we have a country that is worth our boasting; and as sure am I, that, when that day shall come, a new era will be inaugurated, — a golden era, in which the people from the Lakes to the Gulf will have, for the first time, one purpose and one aim. We shall be one people, and come out of the fiery furnace of this great trial cleansed, and renewed in our manhood.

CHAPTER III.

LOUISIANANS.

COULD an angel take his position above any of our great Northern cities, what would he see that would tell him that the people below were engaged in a war mightier in its results than the wars of Alexander and Cæsar? Poising thus mid-heaven, he would see only the swaying crowd asking the price of stocks one minute; and, the next, turning to the list of killed and wounded; and, the next, inquiring again the price of stocks. Be his eye never so clear, he would fail to detect the signs of a great national struggle, either on the wharves or in the busy marts. Only when, with a power granted to angels alone, he should look into our homes, would he discover the terrible shadow which the god of war casts as he stalks through the world. Here, a young wife; one who has known the sacred glory and peace of wedded life for a few short months only; who gave her all without a murmur and without a foreboding; sitting now by her lonely hearth, the fire gone out, and the fire in her heart gone out with it. She sits weeping; for she has a strange, vacant feeling in her soul, which nothing now on earth can fill. She looks with eager eyes at something which she thinks she must see; but it is not there. In sweet forgetfulness, she speaks aloud a loved name; but the sound of her own voice calls her back to the reality: then she covers her face with her hands, and weeps as only such as she can. There, again, is one bent with years. She holds in her trembling hand a letter; and, as her eyes are lifted to the great God who sees all his children, her lips murmur, " He was my only boy, and now I am alone!" There, still again, in her own room, apart from the family, sits a young girl. She has known only the summer-time of life until now; and, as the hot tears fall thick and fast, the angel who looks from his lofty poise sighs in sympathy, and whispers, in such sweet tones that the echo falls upon the sad one's ear, " My child, the good God doeth all things well."

And then the angel casts his eye from these homes of sorrow to the distant fields of Virginia or the West; and there, lying under a tree, the young husband is praying with his last breath for her who is so soon to be a widow. And yonder, lying on his back, cold and bloody, is the fair-haired boy, whose last word was " Mother!" And yonder, again, by that broken cannon, bleeds the brave youth for whom the maiden weeps. He has taken from his bosom a miniature; and as he falls back, giving his body to the earth, he presses the picture to his lips. This is war, and all that we of the North have ever known of it.

Not so in Louisiana. Every thing there reminds you of its destructive power. Three years ago, the river was alive with steamboats. By night, as well as by day, the noise of their paddle-wheels and the screaming of their whistles disturbed your repose. The wharves and the levees groaned with the burden of a great commerce. The streets were filled with drays; and the cursing crowd of drivers gave evidence of plenty of business. The St. Charles was crowded with people from every nation on the globe. But now you can hardly recognize the place. A terrible and fatal palsy has taken hold of the limbs of that giant city. You can run your horse along the wharves and the levee, and through the streets, without danger of collision. It seems as though a plague had fallen upon the doomed city, and all the people had fled in dismay.

The St. Charles is empty. Its vast drinking-room, reminding you that the most important part of a Southern hotel is the bar, echoes your steps like a hall deserted. You may pass along the chief business streets; and, on an average, not one store in five will be open: and the few that are open in the daytime close at dusk; for the custom will not warrant the necessary expenditure for gas.

I was, at first, strangely affected by this appearance of universal stagnation. As I looked round upon the desolation which everywhere prevailed, I could not help crying out in pity, "Alas! Rome is no longer Rome." It was a long time before I could shake off this funereal gloom. I did get bravely over it, however, by asking a few pertinent questions. .

"Whose store is this?".

"It *was* John Brugier's, sir."

"Why do you say *was?*"

"Because he has packed up all his goods, and gone beyond the lines."

The truth was, that every closed shutter was the sign of a rebel; and, as the closed shutters were to the open windows as ten to one, I was forcibly reminded that I was living in a city of traitors, upon whose heels was just coming the punishment of their great crime.

What is the meaning of these marks of fire on the levees, and of those charred planks on the river-bank? They are indications of the places where thousands of cotton-bales were set on fire, and steamboats and river-craft by the dozen, when the Orleanists heard that Ben Butler was coming up the river.

So the levees were empty, and there was no trade on the river; and, in consequence, the people of the city were being put to great straits for a living, because they all hated the old flag which was coming proudly and victoriously up the stream.

I grew to be even glad of the deep gloom; for it seemed to me that the desolation was a richly merited punishment. There was only one class that I pitied, — the class that, left to act according to its true instincts, will always be on the side of republicanism. The poorer people, those who are termed well-to-do, and the laboring multitudes, — these I greatly pitied. They will continue to suffer; and large numbers must be supported by our Government until that auspicious day when peace restores to them the blessed privilege of earning their daily bread.

It seems that the rebels were aware of the Union proclivities of these people, and, even in the hurry and bustle of defeat, did not fail to take their revenge; for, when the enemy's troops were about to evacuate the place, there were many thousands of hogsheads of sugar, and barrels of molasses, to be destroyed. With large sledge-hammers, the men who were detailed for this duty drove the heads of the barrels and hogsheads in; and, when the crowd of poor came with their buckets to save a part of the immense spoils, they were driven away at the bayonet's point. This wanton destruction of property was simply a proof that the South were unconsciously committing suicide. They hate us, the Yankees, not with an honorable, chivalrous hatred, but with a petty spitefulness, which is the characteristic of a small nature engaged in an unworthy cause.

I saw no indications of that heavy gloom, that sullen, lowering, portentous gloom, which fills the heart of the patriot Pole when he feels the tyranny of the Czar. I can conceive of a city brooding in silence over real or fancied wrongs, wrapped in affliction, and filling the atmosphere of every street with most ominous murmurings; but you discover none of that massive, frowning earnestness in New Orleans. The dainty damsel carefully gathers up her skirts as she goes by a Union soldier, or wears a breastpin on which is gaudily painted the rebel flag; the strong man, standing at the corner of the street, mutters something about the damned Yankees; the mob, at dead of night, hurrah for Jeff Davis: that is all. The people of the city, once in a while, splutter a rebel sentiment; but their secessionism is of the pouting, petulant sort, rather than earnest: it is mean and poor-spirited, not grand or noble. It is chiefly shown by the wealthiest in complaints that they cannot run their plantations, and get their usual harvest; and by all others, in deceiving the customs, and smuggling goods beyond our lines, whereby a mint of money is made.

My feeling is, that the poetry and romance of secessionism are all gone. Instead of gloom, which may conceal the most devoted patriotism, you find, among the planters, only disappointment. I have talked with hundreds of them; and, after spending five minutes in discussing the right of the matter, they have invariably ended by hoping that affairs will be so arranged that the " plantations " and the " niggers " can be rendered profitable. It was because the price of negroes was gradually getting so high that the gain on the crop was materially lessened, — dollars and cents, — that all, except the crafty politicians, gave their support to the war. Secessionism was little else than an immense financial speculation, covered up by a vast cumulus of nebulous rhetoric about Southern rights. The only right they cared for was the right to turn human blood into bullion. They chafed, not at any harsh laws which we had imposed, but against the humane sentiment of the age as represented by the people of the Free States. They openly confess that the independence of the South would have opened the African slave-trade. This would have brought the negro's price down to eight hundred dollars, instead of sixteen as it was two years ago; and then the profits of the crop would have been greater.

If you leave the city, and take the level road to Baton Rouge, — a hundred and thirty miles up the river, — the desolation becomes all the more marked. There is not a single planter in the department who has not personally suffered through this war. Their crops of sugar-cane, yielding from five hundred to a thousand hogsheads of sugar, are still standing in February; and there is no hope of saving them, for the frost has been at work on them. I have ridden through miles of plantations, from which only a few hogsheads of sugar had been made. Cane is standing now in March; thousands and tens of thousands of acres of it. Thus the crop of the past year is nothing; and that of the coming year will be the same. The planters' negroes have all fled; their horses have all been stolen, their mules and teams have all been confiscated. They stand in the midst of their great plantations, with the interest on a heavy mortgage staring them in the face, perfectly powerless. Can they get their niggers back? Yes, if they choose to come, — not otherwise; and then they are apprentices, and no longer slaves. Can they recover their teams and mules? Not one. Fifty thousand Union soldiers are somewhere within a hundred miles of them; and their baggage must have transportation, and their food be carried from camp to camp. Uncle Sam, with more than his usual foresight and severity, has pressed into the service of his soldiers the whole mule-force of the department. What, then, is left for the planters to do? How can they pay the demands of angry creditors against their estate?

These are questions a hundred gentlemen have asked me. I have had only one answer, and that was suggested by Dr. Johnson. One day, a wretched vagabond, after exhausting all other arguments in hopes of getting the longed-for charity, cried out surlily, —

"But I must live, sir."

"I don't recognize any such necessity," replied the gruff doctor, and marched on.

"I must carry on my plantation," said one of these sufferers, who are well aware that they are paying a heavy price for the luxury of rebellion.

"Why must you?" I retorted.

"Why must I? Because, if I don't, I can't pay my debts."

"Well, suppose you do not pay your debts: what of it, sir?"

"What of it?" said my irate friend, — "what of it, sir? Why, I shall starve, and all my family will be reduced to poverty. Three years ago, I was worth a million; now, not a picayune."

"Exactly," I replied; "and what, pray, does the United-States Government *care*, whether you, who for two years have stood in opposition to it, are worth a picayune or not? If you are a beggar, put it down as the legitimate result of rebellion."

DOLLARS AND CENTS.

That man voted for the act of secession, and grew eloquent as he dilated on the glories of Southern independence, and detailed the tyrannies of the North. He gave five thousand dollars to the cause, and publicly pledged his life. Now he is willing to take a round hundred oaths of allegiance for the sake of a few mules and teams.

The war is really a terrible burden to the South. We are afflicted in our sympathies and our affections: they have, superadded to this, a heavy affliction in the pocket. Their whole country is running wild: it is impossible to hope for any crops. So the enemy either sits down in despair, passive, because powerless; or, enraged, cuts the levee, and floods and destroys the plantations for miles around. It will require many, many years to restore the country between New Orleans and Baton Rouge to its ancient position of plenty and thrift.

But, besides all this, there is the work of the cannon-ball to be reckoned. Not only is the trade of the entire department checked, and not only are its crops destroyed, but its towns, many of them, have been more or less injured. Baton Rouge has lost its magnificent State House: nothing but the outer frame of brick-work remains. The splendid statue of Washington (by Powers) was saved; and that is all. The costly furniture and the elegant library, said to have been one of the finest in the country, were completely demolished. Its works of art, collected at vast expense, — the result of many years of labor, — all have disappeared. Within those walls, in 1861, were heard words of burning eloquence from some of the most gifted sons of the State, inciting the people of Louisiana to rebellion. Men who had been taught to revere the past history of republicanism now dared to point the finger of scorn at it. The old flag, which had floated over every sea, protecting Southern commerce; that had been won by the mingled life-blood of Northerner and Southerner, who forgot partisan feeling, and fought for human liberty, — the old flag was laughed to bitter scorn, and tossed into the dirt. This was done in the State capitol, which now lies in ruins. Yes: it was done in the presence of that statue, which Northern genius had carved, of him who was not only a Virginian, but an American. Surely they must have known that the sacrilege would be avenged.

In 1862, the old flag met the new flag face to face. The battle was fought within the very shadow of that senate-chamber. Williams bravely led on his men, and fell. Nothing daunted, Cahill and Dudley, who are every inch soldiers, gathered their forces, and, making a determined onset while the bullets were flying like hail-stones, drove the new flag away, and planted the old flag — the only flag of the American — in its accustomed place over the State capitol. It must have waved proudly there while the stars and bars crept behind the horizon in the distance. But all was not over, even then. The recreant building was fired; and, while the flames were spreading, the one thing that was saved was the statue that had been a silent witness of the treason which had been plotted for many months. It seemed then as though justice was satisfied. The framework of the building stands to-day, looking gloomily down on the river, — a wreck of former grandeur, and a prophecy of the end of the Rebellion.

The little town of Donaldsonville, too, is a sufferer. Our gunboats were frequently fired upon by the guerillas belonging to the place. Gen. Butler bore the outrage until forbearance ceased to be a virtue; and then assured the people, that, if it were again committed, he would shell the town. It was again committed; and, I need not add, the gunboats did their duty. It afterwards became necessary to get rid of a large number of brick buildings which stood in the way of our artillery; and, consequently, they were destroyed. There is about half of the original town left. Many of the inhabitants have fled; and, were it not for the presence of our troops, the place would be lonely enough. All who had the power and the money fled at once to the rebel lines. Those left were mostly poor Creoles, Spanish, French, and German, who were almost to a man Unionists. They have been of great service to us as guides, and in giving us valuable information.

This class of Louisianians, the Creoles, is made up of people whose peculiarities demand a somewhat extended notice. There is the poor and the rich Creole. The rich one is, perhaps, the bitterest enemy to the cause of the North that can be found. He is virulent in his hatred, and will stop at no bounds. He will utter his treason in spite of the law. You may take his slaves, his teams, his crop, his house, and leave him a beggar; still he will not flinch. He is the enemy of the flag, and glories in it. He is the only man in the South, the politician and demagogue excepted, who is really willing to sacrifice every thing for the sake of the cause. He

8

was born on the soil. He has hot blood in his veins. He is full of ignorance and prejudice. The chances are, that he is not a person of any education. He has not the undisputed *entrée* into the highest circles. He is regarded, socially, with suspicion by his wealthy neighbors, and with something like envy and hatred by the poor. He is, generally, a hard, pinching master; a sycophant in the presence of those higher, a tyrant over those below him. He knows nothing of the North; for he reads little. He cannot calmly discuss the issues of the hour; for he has never thought of them. He has given himself to the war, because of an inherent hatred of abolitionists.

When you talk to another of the institution, he will blandly and plausibly argue concerning its divinity, assert its missionary influence, and adduce facts to prove that free labor will never succeed at the South; but, beneath it all, you see that the man has twisted himself into such a belief. His instincts are all the other way. His interest has warped him. Change the direction of the interest, and, presto! you have a good abolitionist.

Not so with the Creole. A love of slavery is in the marrow of his bones. He says he has so many "head of niggers," as he speaks of his cattle. He never talks to you of slavery as a missionary society. That is the stronghold of one who does not believe what he asserts. He never offers any statistics to prove that free labor is impracticable. He stands on a platform beneath which are no such subterfuges. He simply says, —

" The nigger, sir, was intended by Almighty God to be the slave of the white man. He isn't a man: he belongs to a lower order of being."

" But, sir," you commence to reply.

" There are no ' buts ' about it. I have lived fifty years with them. I know them through and through ; and nothing is more evident to a sane man, than that the nigger is one grade only above the ape."

This is refreshing. There is no chance for argument. You are simply dealing with a fanatic of the worst and most unreasonable kind. He is worshipping his ebony idol with all the blind devotion of the East Indian. He is not a man of the nineteenth century, but shows all the characteristics of a semi-barbarous age. He resists the Government at every point.

Just beyond Carrollton is an immense and magnificent estate owned by one of these Creoles. His annual yield of sugar is fifteen hundred hogsheads. He might have taken the oath of allegiance, and thus saved his property ; but he would not. The work of depredation commenced ; but he bore it without a murmur. First we took his wagons, harnesses, and mules: he said nothing, but scowled most awfully. Next we emptied his stables of horses for the cavalry service; he did not have even a pony left, and was compelled to trudge along on foot: still nothing was said. Next we took his entire crop, ground it in his own sugar-house, used his barrels for the molasses, and his hogsheads for the sugar, and marked the head of each "U. S.:" not a murmur. Then his negroes, three hundred and more, house-servants and all, took it into their woolly heads to come within our camp-lines. The Creole was most completely stripped: still he stood in the midst of the ruins, damning Abe Lincoln, and wishing that he had eight instead of four sons in the rebel army.

He is our only enemy in the South for whom I have any respect. He is the only man who is terribly in earnest. He has thrown every thing into the dice-box, and is willing to meet the result. While others are intriguing to get from the commanding general some new concession, he sits under his gallery, moody, ugly, dangerous. In degenerate times like these, an earnest friend is the best thing to see; but the next best thing is an earnest enemy.

The poor Creoles, the only Union men of the South, except the negroes, are an entirely different kind of people. They are the social victims of the institution. They are looked down upon and trodden upon by every other class in society.

"Why should I love the South?" said one to me in a moment of confidence; "and why should I uphold slavery? I am a poor man, and there is no possibility of my ever becoming any thing else. I am an overseer; but Mr. B—— will not let me go into his parlor, nor will he allow me to sit at his table. I am just as much a slave as though I were black."

"But suppose slavery were abolished?"

"Why, then society would be different. Public opinion would help me. It would not be simply slaves and masters: it would be the wealthy, the working-class, and the poor. There is no ladder now up which I can climb: there would be one then."

He knew just where he stood, and the reason why he stood there.

Again: when our forces were on the march towards Opelousas, I rode over one of the magnificent prairies to a small white house, which offered a quiet retreat for the night. The proprietor was a Creole, who owned a farm of some two hundred acres, and fifty or sixty head of cattle. When, at nightfall, I seated myself on the gallery, I noticed that he was walking back and forth in great trepidation.

" Mr. Botin, what is the trouble?"

" Oh, dear! oh, dear! I was only damning Gov. Mouton!"

" That is good Christian work, certainly; and I hope you will find relief in it. But, prithee, why do you damn that good rebel?"

" Because I voted for him, and he has ruined me," he replied very dolefully.

" Why did you vote for him?"

" Oh! we poor Creoles couldn't help it. He got us all in a large hall, and told us he would get us rid of the United States, and we should all be rich men. I made objections against many of his measures; but his friends only said, ' Oh! he will fix all that when he is Governor:' so we voted for him, and now we are ruined."

It is easy to see that the State of Louisiana was lost because there were no newspapers to regulate public opinion, and no public education, which teaches the poor man to think for himself.

" Oh! the candidate will fix all that when he is elected," would not satisfy the New-England farmer.

I have never been so surprised in my life as I was at the discovery of the vast amount of ignorance among the poorer classes. You may travel twenty miles from almost any central point, and find neither schoolhouse nor church. You may enter twenty houses of small farmers, and not find a single book. The humble classes neither read, write, nor think. Indeed, the impression one receives in going among the peasantry of the South is, that they belong to a past age, or to one of the older countries, and certainly not to this most brilliant century, which boasts of nothing so much as of its unlimited means of education.

Once in a while, society is called upon to pay the score. Near Franklin, or within a circle of fifty miles from that centre, are some three hundred Arizonians, — a population that could exist only in the South. They are owners of small farms, ignorant, unprincipled, treacherous. Everybody lifts his hand against them, and their hands strike at everybody's face. Lately, they joined in solemn league to befriend each other in case of difficulty, to resist the conscript act, and to live on their neighbors. They were a motley crew, all good shots, and all determined not to enter the army. One night, four fine horses were stolen from the ample stables of George Barker. After great trouble, they were traced to the humbler barn of one John Solin. When the said John was asked how he came by the horses, he quietly said that he had owned them about five years; and, to prove his assertion, he brought them out, and exhibited his private mark on the shoulder of each.

Of course, George Barker was thunder-struck. He had supposed, that, when the property was found, the poor devil of an Arizonian would go down on his knees, beg off, and promise never to do, or rather be found doing, the like again.

After some parley, the said John was marched off to jail ; and, the next day, four neighbors solemnly swore that they recognized the horses by well-known marks, and that they belonged to George Barker. Judge of the surprise, not only of George, but also of his four rich neighbors, when the placid John brought into court twenty Arizonians, each of whom most solemnly swore that they, too, recognized the said horses, and that, to their certain knowledge, John Solin had owned them during the last five years !

The members of this society would have sworn any thing, however preposterous. They did not know the value of an oath, nor did they have the slightest fear of perjury.

The court was reluctantly compelled to decide that the visual organs of George and his four rich neighbors were out of order, while placid John carried his noble horses home in triumph.

These marauders rendered the country unsafe for many miles around. At last, when the whole police force of the district were set on their track, they retired to an island of upland in the middle of a floating prairie. It was a perfect, natural stronghold. This floating prairie consists of finely-knit and knotted roots, about eighteen inches in thickness, which have entirely covered the surface of a lake. Cut through this mat, and you come to water, as in the North you cut through the ice with the same result. It is dangerous to travel over these prairies, unless you are well acquainted with the path. As you walk along, the unsteady sod gives beneath your feet; and, if you should fall through, there is no hope. No horse or carriage can pass over them.

It was to such a place as this that the Arizonians retired : and if, by chance, some luckless policeman fell into their hands, he was treated as a natural enemy, and put to death; or if one of the party ventured home for a few days, and was caught, no bribes nor threats could induce him to discover to the officers of justice the firm paths over the floating prairie. He might, for a stipulated sum, promise to do this, and would lead an armed band hither and thither until night came, and the whole party were worn out; then quietly slip away on some path known only to himself to laugh with his comrades, while the duped officers were left to enjoy their chagrin at defeat.

Vigilance-committees were organized to take the law into their own hands. But little has been accomplished thus far. The Arizonians still ply their trade, and stand as faithfully by each other as ever did Spanish bandits or Italian highwaymen.

This account of the Arizonians is literally true; and I am willing to assert, that it is an anomaly in American society, which is possible only in the South. Nor is it possible there, because it is an agricultural region; and because, therefore, the means of education are limited. So is the West agricultural; and yet it is impossible to suppose the existence of such a society in Northern Indiana or in Wisconsin. It could exist only among a people who have failed to erect a standard of right, and whose public opinion is not moral or high-toned.

There is a little colony of this same class of people at the Pass, at the mouth of the Mississippi. They are among the most ignorant, debased, and vile set of men to be found on the earth. The other day, one of my friends, a Northern man, whose vessel was detained for some time at the Pass by stress of weather, conceived the benevolent design of speaking to these people upon the subject of religion. I should shock my readers, were I to attempt to describe the perfect mental and spiritual desolation which existed among these people. Still, one anecdote must not be lost. After my friend had talked with a number of stragglers, he entered one of the low huts, and began to converse with the ancient dame. Soon four sons came in, and joined in the conversation; then the old man, the patriarch. He was the only one who made any pretensions to know any thing of God or duty.

My friend spoke of the Lord. He told of his sufferings, and at last exclaimed, —

"And it was he, the dear Son of God, you know, who died that we all might live."

The family all stared. The patriarch alone failed to be startled. Leaning forward, and putting his right hand behind his right ear to enable him to catch every sound, he cried out, —

"Mister! did you say it was the *Son* of God who died?"

"Yes, my friend; and he died on the cross."

"You are sure it was the Son?"

"Yes. Why?"

"Oh, nothin'! only I allers thought it was the *old man!*"

This anecdote is sacrilegious; but it bespeaks a degree of moral depravity and of woful ignorance such as can be found in only two places, — in the South and in Central Africa.

All the Creoles in the State, who are worth less than twenty thousand dollars, desire the success of the Northern arms. They were carried into the war per force, and it has only ruined them. Their sons have been conscripted, and are deserting every day ; hoping for nothing so much as to get back to the quietness of the farm. They will tell you plainly, that the war is for the protection of the rich planters, and that they are unwilling to risk their lives in any such cause. To prove this, we have but to look at a few facts. It is beyond question, that when the matter of secession was discussed, and the people of Louisiana were appealed to, to follow in the footsteps of her illustrious sister, South Carolina, one hundred and fifty-eight delegates were sent to the State Convention ; and, of that number, a very large majority had pledged themselves to the people to vote for a continuance in the Union. They were sent for that special purpose. This is sufficient to show how the body of voters felt at that critical moment. Again: when the first vote was taken in the State Convention, it resulted as the people desired it should, and greatly to the chagrin of that nondescript biped known as a " lobbyist." The bipeds were not, however, discouraged. They knew with whom they had to deal. One after another, the delegates began to see the other side ; and the loyalists were evidently losing ground. Money, promises, and threats were doing their work ; and yet, when the vote was taken, which was expected to be

final, and when the New-Orleans editors were so
sure of the result that they announced the passage
of the act of secession by an overwhelming majority, and the people were in consternation, at that
very time the real vote stood three majority in
favor of the Union. It took the lobbyists some
three weeks to buy the requisite number of votes
to put the matter beyond reasonable question.
This is the way Louisiana went out of the Union.
It was only by a long pull, a strong pull, and a pull
altogether, on the part of the slave-owners and
their pimps, against the feelings, the sense of justice, and the patriotism of the people.

After that, they held meetings in every village,
and succeeded by fables and lies in imbittering
the mind of the poorer classes against the North.
Had there been a middle estate, firm, independent,
thoughtful, "who knew their rights, and, knowing,
dared maintain," as there is in the North, Louisiana would to-day be true and loyal; but because
slavery allows no middle estate, and has precluded
the possibility of popular education, the credulous
people have been utterly ruined.

I will venture to say, that of the fifty-six hundred who answered to their names at roll-call at
Berwick's Bay, when our forces chased the enemy
into Texas, more than one thousand fell behind
their column on the march to Opelousas for the

sole purpose of being taken. They were mostly conscripts, and joined the army with the intention of deserting at the first opportunity. I had a long chat with many a squad that had been sent to the rear; and they told me that they were sick and tired of the army, and that they were glad to be taken, because they could go back to their families and farms.

" Yes; but, boys, haven't you any patriotism? Aren't you willing to fight for the glorious South?"

"We are not fighting for the South. We have never been disturbed. We always got along well enough. The truth is, we are all fighting for the rich planters, and not for ourselves."

" Yes," said another, " we are fighting for the niggers; and their masters hire them to the Government, to work on trenches, for eighteen dollars a month; while we sleep out of doors, and get nothing to eat, and clothe ourselves, for eleven dollars."

" They are terribly afraid a nigger will get killed," said another; " and then they lose their money. When there is prospect of a fight, they take all the niggers off out of harm's way: but they don't care for us; we didn't cost any thing. So, for one, I am going to care for myself. I only hope the Yankees will kill every planter in the State. Then we shall have peace."

I never expected to hear one native-born in the South say that this Rebellion is simply due to slaveholders and politicians.

Many of these men have taken up arms on our side, and thus proved the truth of my criticism. There are, I believe, four regiments made up of those who have, in some way or other, been persecuted by the South. They consist of poor Creoles, generally deserters, and Spanish, French, and German citizens, many of whom took to the woods, and lived there for weeks, in order to avoid the conscription act. These form an important portion of the troops in the department, and deserve particular mention. They are the most savage-looking set of men I ever laid eyes on. Their *morale* is, of course, very low; but, with strict discipline, they will make splendid soldiers. They are just such men as compose the regular army, — persons who are desperate, and who have been urged by some unusual fortune to this step. In the slight services which they have as yet been called upon to perform, they have shown great promptness and willingness.

The First Louisiana particularly attracted my attention. Twenty-seven different nationalities are represented in it. Every spot on the globe, from China to Peru, seems to have sent its quota to fill up the ranks.

Here is the poor Chinaman, with his half-moon eyes, a contented body, into whose mind the idea of preferment never comes. Here, again, is the sharp Jew, who has travelled over the whole of Europe, and will talk to you in any one of a dozen languages; or, if you prefer, he is ready to barter with you for your uniform. There, standing against the tree, is a tall, stalwart Hungarian. His bushy beard covers his face; but it is rumored that he has been through a dozen battles already, and knows enough of military science to command a regiment: still he is only a corporal. There, again, is a rough Teuton, who, like Nelson, does not know who Fear is. A dozen like him have been mounted; and, when there is any scouting to be done, they are always ready. Yonder, again, pounding in the mortar with his big pestle, is a tough, wiry little fellow, with nothing about him that would attract attention; yet I am told that he carries " Euripides " in his pocket as a *vade-mecum*, and that he is thoroughly posted in all the branches of medical science. These men have been through strange experiences; and could you sit by the side of each for an hour, when the right mood was on him, he could tell you stories more like fiction than reality.

The regiment is a queer conglomerate. There are those who doubt their value as troops on the field; but their officers place great trust in them. It may be that few of them are fired with as warm enthusiasm for the cause as Northern soldiers : still they all meet on one platform, — implacable hatred of the rebels. It is a feeling which arises greatly from the fact, that they have suffered impressment; which has been increased by the other fact, of desertion. It resembles, in many respects, the old feeling between the Jacobins and the Loyalists in France. They have been kept down by the usages of society. They have chafed at it; and now the chance is offered, not only of successful resistance, but also of revenge. My own feeling is, that they will fight like tigers ; that they will commit any depredation, and every conceivable one, on the foe.

On the whole, I was not much affected by that awe with which we are told by many to approach the gentleman of the South. I have spent months upon the plantations of the State, and have met the planters, very many of them, on friendly terms, in the midst of their own households ; and I confess to great disappointment. I am willing to aver as the result of my experience, that there is no class of society in the South which is equal in its culture, its refinement of manner and of taste, and its enjoyment of life, to the same class in the North. After the immense number of traditions which have been handed down to us, each lauding the Southerner as a perfect Chesterfield in outward demeanor, and a prodigal in his open-handed generosity, I may seem somewhat rash in making this statement. I can only say, that if you will approach the idol, and examine closely, you will find that the marble look is but varnish after all, and that the thing is made of common wood.

I will say further, that the planters of the South are not equal as a body, from any point of view, to the well-to-do merchants of the North. I know that such a statement is rank heresy. From our childhood, we have been taught to think differently. I remember, that, years ago, this matter puzzled me. I put in the one scale all the *à priori* arguments I could collect, — that a society, in which the individuals were each insulated, must, logically, degenerate ; that it is not favorable to literature, religion, or manliness ; and, in the other scale, I placed this weighty public opinion. The former always kicked the beam. But now I know that my logic was correct, and that the world's rhetoric was false.

Indeed, why should this not be true ? There is not the same rivalry in the South that there is with us. The influence of the whole life and of all the surroundings of the planter is to dull him, to warp his judgment, to make him selfish. He lives in and on himself. On the other hand, the Northerner, coming in daily contact with men engaged in constant rivalries with him, becomes not simply self-reliant and prejudiced, as the Southerner does, who lives in necessary solitude, but self-reliant and generous. He is well posted on all matters. He reads, thinks, and talks a great deal.

Here is another side of the Southern character, which was exposed by my intimate relations with the planters. I have always been led to suppose that the Yankee is peculiar, in that he will sacrifice more for a silver dollar than any other biped of the *genus homo*. In strong contrast stands the open-handed and large-hearted Southerner. "There is nothing small south of Mason and Dixon's line," says the copperhead. So the shrivelled Yankee stands opposite the chivalrous Southerner; the one giving a three-cent piece, the other a bright eagle, to the poor beggar-girl.

I do not doubt that the Southerner spends an eagle to every three-cent piece which the Yankee expends in the cause of street-girls; though the gift is hardly one that would be sanctioned by the Church. But, in real generosity, the Southerner is far behind the Northerner. The South has acquired a reputation for a reckless carelessness of money; but it is all built on the fact, that the people never take any change for a picayune. There is a certain devil-may-care way about them, which

gives you the impression that they never saw any
thing so small as a one-dollar bill. They are always
turning criticism away from themselves by letting
their wit and sarcasm fly at honest Northerners.
Once a year, they gather together all their new
clothes and all their jewelry, and take some Northern hotel by assault; run up large bills for car-
riages and wine; throw down a quarter for a ten-
cent cigar; and, when the counter-jumper offers
the change, turn up their noses, as though it was
a vulgar habit to take change for any thing. That
is the way they get their reputation. But look in
on them during the rest of the year. For nine
months, a planter is on his plantation. The nearest
neighbor is from two to five miles distant. He has
only the tame excitement which a farmer's life
allows. He has three hundred negroes. He gives
them, for a house, a hut, which no man can live in
two years, without becoming thoroughly demoralized. He gives them, for food, so many ears of corn,
which they are to shell, and pound into meal, in a
mortar made of the trunk of a tree, hollowed out;
and so many pounds of bacon, so hard that a respectable dog would refuse to eat it. These negroes
are owned — I use the word in its broadest sense,
as the proportion of mulattoes on every plantation abundantly proves — by the master, who can,
when the caprice moves him, or when he gets up

of a morning out of temper through the last night's wine, give them fifty or a hundred lashes. They work from early morning to late evening, and hardly ever get any pay for service rendered. The master makes the first outlay for his hands. After that, their cost is merely nominal. I never yet have seen a field-hand who was not in rags, and I have seen from twenty to thirty thousand: so the cost of clothing cannot be much. Now, I would like to know where the chivalry, high-mindedness, and other qualities of mind and heart, which are claimed for Southerners, are to be discovered. So far as my experience goes, — and it is abundantly corroborated by the testimony of the provost-marshals of every parish between Fort Jackson and Baton Rouge, — a more shrewd and grasping population cannot be found anywhere. To be sure, there are honorable exceptions. The South produces many polished gentlemen; but when it is asserted, as it has been by Vice-President Stephens, that the Southerners are a race of gentlemen, I must confess, that, if it is so, the planters of Louisiana and the prisoners which have been taken have become greatly demoralized since 1861.

If they were really a generous, chivalrous, and patriotic people, fighting only for the sacred cause of liberty, instead of a fanatical people, completely demoralized by their social institutions, would it be possible for them to adopt such measures as they have adopted towards unoffending Union citizens? I can conceive of a populace completely thrilled by a single purpose, who should frown out of sight, or at least into deep silence, all who opposed their purpose; I can conceive of the swelling tide of secessionism pouring through the streets, and compelling every Union man to keep within doors: but it is beyond belief, that any people, not demoralized, should use means so barbarous to rid themselves of obnoxious individuals. Only in a community where the moral standard indicates zero can such outrages be committed as those which have been well authenticated. Secessionism seems simply to have given license to all the hitherto-restrained passions of society; to have crazed sober-minded men; and to have turned the community so completely upside-down, that it has lost its balance: and its history is being written by its ruffians, its wild, untamed hoosiers, rather than by its heroes and sages. There are scenes, which are undoubted, so disgraceful, that they stamp with infamy any community wherein they have occurred. I know, that, in times of revolution, one ought not to expect the same restraint which is the best blessing of peace. I know, that, in the last century, there were scenes enacted which will never reflect honor upon us.

Ruffians were not wanting, who used the confusion of the times as a cover for their own evil practices. But we all know the severity which Burr in Westchester visited upon these scoundrels; and yet their crime consisted only in breaking open private houses, and robbing the inmates. It was robbery, whose incentive was simply a thirst for gain.

In the present case, the act is different, as is also the motive. It is not the simple plunder of private property which entails such disgrace on the Southern cause: it is the brutal, yes, fiendish treatment of old men, and even of women and children. Scenes have been enacted in some of the Southern States, which would have called a blush to the faces of the French populace in 1789. Is it thus, I ask, that the chivalry show their love of independence? Are they not satisfied with the common excitements of camp-life, that they must ferret out like bloodhounds the old man who spent his youth with the giants of the glorious past, and who dares to speak his mind to the pygmies of the inglorious present? Are there not Yankees enough to kill, that they must satisfy their thirst for blood by torturing women and children? Is it patriotism, is it loyalty to any thing but the infernal institution, which prompts them to such valorous deeds? There is a spitefulness, a rancor, a thirst for vengeance, in the Southern heart, which is very hard to account for.

I had occasion, in January last, to visit some hundred or more Texans, who had succeeded in escaping to our lines. Most of them were from Houston or Austin, owners of cattle and farms.

" Why did you not remain quietly at home ? " I said to one of them.

" Because the rebels burned down our houses, and threatened to hang us if we did not leave within four and twenty hours."

" But they would not have hung you."

One of them, a bright youth, stepped up to me, and said with quivering lips, —

" They did hang my old father; and I was compelled to look on, and see it done."

I have never seen men more incensed. They had lost every cent of their property, brought with them only what they stood in, led their wives hundreds of miles through by-woods and swamps, and only asked to be led back in force. Their cheeks burned; for each had his separate tale of persecution. Their lips quivered; and, as they cursed the secessionists, their oaths seemed to come up from the core of their hearts.

A dozen men in a village meet in a convenient bar-room, and constitute themselves a vigilance-committee. After having filled themselves with whiskey, they sally forth to the house of some unfortunate victim. Him they find in the midst of his family. They enter, and proceed on their unhallowed mission. The father is, perhaps, brutally shot in the presence of his wife and little ones. His wife and daughters are polluted by the touch of these fiends, and can never hold up their heads in honor again. They are turned from their own doors, and look back from the neighboring hill upon the fiery scene of desolation and the grave of a husband and a father. What, I ask, will the future historian say of such things? He cannot blind himself to them. They are not scattered so far apart that he can ignore them: they cluster about the villages of every State, — lurid flames of crime. And what can we say of the people in whose midst such things are tolerated? Could they happen in any one of the Free States? Not even the excess of ruffianism which swept through Kansas could rouse the free part of that State to such infamous deeds. The glory belongs to the South alone. It is only the chivalry, when waging war to defend an institution which has completely demoralized and ruined them, who can quench all pity, and all pure love of woman, and call that patriotism which others call infamy.

One of those atrocities, which serve as thermometers to show that the moral mercury is far out of sight and below the freezing-point, was committed almost in our very presence. Col. Dwight had been sent from Opelousas, where the main body of the army had bivouacked, to Washington, some six miles beyond. We had met with no resistance. The inhabitants, quietly though sullenly, submitted to the Federal triumph. It became necessary to send a messenger from headquarters to communicate with the general. Capt. Dwight, a young man of great promise, of quiet dignity of character, and of sterling integrity, was chosen for the task. It should have been a task attended with no danger whatever. The country through which he was to travel — and there was but the high-road to ride in — would, under ordinary circumstances and among a civilized people, be as safe as the turnpike from Boston to Brookline. So little did he apprehend danger, that he took no weapon whatever. He had advanced about half-way, when he struck some woods, and was hurrying on, when three men appeared in the middle of the road, and commanded a "halt." Reining up his horse, he demanded their business. They gave some insolent reply; when he saw the predicament he was in, and, supposing that he had fallen into an ambush, said quietly, —

"Well, I have no means of defending myself, and must yield as your prisoner;" at the same time, alighting from his horse.

"We don't take any prisoners. Kill the damned Yankee!" was the reply.

At this, one of the ruffians drew a pistol, and shot Dwight in the leg; then another fired, killing him instantly. It was a brutal, ruffianly, unjustifiable murder. It was done in cold blood, and by men who knew what they were about. It was an act that is possible only in a community whence manliness and all the chivalry have long since fled, and only the most debased passions have supplied their place; and yet this is not an insulated instance of cruelty. They are scattered all along the bloody track of this war. They are omnipotent witnesses against Southern society. They tell us that the war has not come an hour too soon. Reform is needed; and the war is the besom which is to sweep the filth from the Southern house.

Every thing that I have seen makes me sure that the cause of the North will triumph. It is the cause of God and of mankind. There is inherent in Southern society, and in the machinery in motion to accomplish the desired result, the prophecy of failure. No people ever disturbed a nation with so little cause. No people ever resorted to so many artifices to support their alleged rights. I feel hopeful that the beginning of the end is at hand. The Confederacy is pretty well worn out. It is now clearly enough proved that the heart of the people is being gradually loosened from the influence of the large land-owners and the politicians, and will be ready in good time to open itself to a holier reverence for the old flag, outside whose benignant shadow it has never known peace or joy.

Let but the North be still a unit, a magnificent unit; let it be patient a little longer; let it keep up its faith in the Providence that is leading us through this struggle; let it demand that all its ministers of vengeance shall act with promptness and energy, not seeking to conciliate, but determined to conquer; let it pour out its wealth a little longer, and tell its sons to tarry yet a little while on the bloody field; let, in one word, the whole North act with decision, and a firm, unwavering belief in the ultimate triumph of republicanism, — and the clouds will be sure to roll away; the good old flag, the flag of Washington and of liberty, covered with powder and glory, will wave proudly over a people who have been tried with fire and the sword, and found faithful.

CHAPTER IV.

THE NEGRO.

AFTER a long day's hard riding over a road made infinitely dusty by an interminable wagon‑train, I came upon a house which seemed to promise a good night's rest for man and beast. I was hungry as well as tired; and though I indulged in the faint hope of fresh meat and flour-bread, and a cup of real Mocha, instead of that wretched counterfeit made out of burnt sugar, in which the members of the Confederacy so largely indulge since the blockade, I nevertheless was morally certain that I should have to make myself contented with a slice of hard ham, and a square of the inevitable corn-cake which has been the staff of life to the rebels ever since the blockade. I (when I say " I," I mean we ; for my friend Wheelock shared these luminous experiences) knocked at the large front-door ; and was very soon confronted by the mistress, to whom the frequent question was put, —

" Madam, may we trespass on your hospitality for the night ? "

The " Yes, I suppose so," came out very reluctantly, and showed plainly enough the proclivities of the landlady.

There was, however, no hesitancy on our part to accept such coldly given succor : for we knew, that, only the week before, the same house had been the favorite rendezvous for rebel officers ; and felt that what had been given to the red, white, and red, was due to the red, white, and blue. She was alone, of course ; and, had I been three months younger, I should have pitied her forlorn and seemingly widowed condition, and checked the exodus of chickens, geese, and turkeys from her barnyard, which threatened soon to leave her destitute of these valuable domestic songsters. But the last three months had added largely to my experience, as well as something to my age ; and, knowing well the occasion of her temporary widowhood, I could find in my heart no spark of pity. Her husband, a Northern recreant, had, a few days before, gathered together his best hands (the young, strong-limbed men), his finest horses, and all his mules, and started for the prairie near Alexandria, whose soil the foot of the Yankee, he thought, would never desecrate.

We found in the Têche a large number of widows of this description. The husbands, sure that they would find no security in the presence of the

Union forces, left their wives and children to the mercy of the invading army, while they themselves sought a safe asylum, with whatever valuable portables they could take with them, within the Confefederate lines.

We promised to keep the house of our unwilling hostess free from stragglers during our stay, — for which favor she seemed very thankful, as this gormandizing rear - guard of the army had spread terror in every kitchen of any promise whatever, — and then retired to our rooms for rest and sleep.

There is such a thing as a weariness too great for sleep; and, after tumbling over my bed restlessly for an hour, I got up, impelled by desperation, and began fumbling over the few books in the room for something to read. I knew, that if I could find something that would interest me, and thus compel me to concentrate my thoughts, — for, when one is overworn, he seems to lose all control over his mind, which plays leap-frog with every conceivable fancy, and wanders restlessly through every zone of Fairy-land, — I should soon reach my goal of sleep.

For a while, I was unsuccessful. Only some remarkable piece of literature could effect the object in view; and, after hopelessly turning over the commonplace pages of a dozen books, I took

up a straggling but providential number of De
Bow's "Review," which lay dusty and dog-eared
under a pile of old secesh newspapers.   The first
article attracted my notice ; and I inwardly cried,
" Eureka ! "   The longed-for sedative was found at
last.   It was so remarkable a paper, that I devoured it with a mental greediness which surprised
even myself; and, when I got to the end, I felt
that it should not be allowed to die.   I determined,
first of all, to sleep on my discovery, and so placed
the volume carefully under my pillow ; and, second,
to perform a labor of love towards the author, and
present it, at least in part, to my friends of the
North.

It appears, from a note which is prefixed to the
paper, that certain gentlemen of Mississippi were
desirous of ascertaining the opinion of the Rev.
Samuel A. Cartwright of New Orleans on the
mooted question of the unity of the races.   Flattered, no doubt, by their kind attentions, the
reverend gentleman, who was probably a slave-
owner, or whose wealthiest parishioners were such,
retired to his study, and in due time emerged with
this very carefully prepared document, purporting
to settle this vexed ethnological question for the
planters of the South.   Being a little timid by
nature, he seemed unwilling to base his arguments
upon facts of character and anatomy, but dis-
coursed thus : —

"Let us, therefore, abandon the slow, uncertain, and tortuous paths of proud science, and seek to know what God has revealed on the subject. If we take the Hebrew Bible for a guide, and faithfully interpret it, there can be but one opinion on the question. That book positively affirms that there were at least two races of intellectual creatures, with immortal souls, created at different times. Thus in the twenty-fourth verse of the first chapter of Genesis: ' The Lord said, Let the earth bring forth *intellectual creatures with immortal souls* after their kind, cattle and creeping thing and beast of the earth after his kind; and it was so.' In our English version, instead of ' *intellectual creatures with immortal souls,*' we have only the words ' *living creatures,*' as representing the Hebrew words *naphesh chayah.* The last word means ' living creature ;' and the word *naphesh,* which invests *chayah,* or living creature, with intellectuality and immortality, is not translated at all, either in the Douay Bible or that of King James. But there it stands, more durable than brass or granite, inviting us to look at the negro and the Indian, and then to look at that, and we will understand it.

"Neither the Catholic nor the Protestant translators of the Bible seem to have had the negroes in their mind's eye when they were looking at the

11

words *naphesh chayah;* or, if they had, they took for granted that they were white men, whose skins a tropical sun had blacked; and hence omitted to translate the words which embrace them. Mississippi and Louisiana are half full of negroes, and so is the Hebrew Bible; but our English version has not got a negro in it.

"The translators surely thought there must be some mistake in regard to the *intellectuality and immortality* of any earthly beings created before Adam, and hence omitted to express the idea of intellectuality and immortality which the original attached to such beings. After the inferior races or inferior *naphesh chayah* were created, God said, 'Let us make Adam (or a superior race of *naphesh chayah*) in our own image, and after our likeness, and let him have dominion over all things on the earth;' including the negroes, of course. Chapter second, verse seventh, says that Adam 'became *a living soul,*'—became a *naphesh chayah.* We understand by *living soul* a creature with intelligence and immortal mind. If the same words had been translated in the same way in the twenty-fourth verse of the first chapter, we should have recognized two creations of intellectual and immortal beings at different times; but these words, being merely rendered *living creatures* in the twenty-fourth verse, confounded the inferior *naphesh chayah* with the brutes mentioned in the same verse.

"Fifty years ago, Dr. Adam Clarke, the learned commentator of the Bible, from deep reading in the Hebrew, Arabic, and Coptic languages, was forced to the conclusion, that the creature that beguiled Eve was an animal formed like man, walked erect, and had the gifts of speech and reason. He believed it was an orang-outang, and not a serpent. *If he had lived in Louisiana, instead of England, he would have recognized the negro gardener.* Eve was a new-comer, and had evidently been questioning, out of curiosity, the gardener, about the tree with the forbidden fruit. The *ophidian Bimana* begins his reply to her questions with an exclamation of astonishment, rendered 'Ay' in our version; equivalent to 'Is it possible?' 'Can it be that Elohim has said you are not to eat of every tree in the garden? Ye shall not die; but, in the day you eat thereof, you will be as gods, knowing good and evil.'

"We are told in the nineteenth verse of the second chapter, that all the creatures were brought before Adam to receive names; and that what he called every living creature, that was the name thereof. What these names were, appears afterward. The names he gave, very often contained an abridged history of the thing itself, shut up in the name, — a sealed book to those who did not know the thing, and intended so to be, until, perhaps, thousands of years' experience had enabled man to acquire the key of knowledge to unlock and read the book.

" The first one of these names, enclosing within the name or history of the thing named, occurs in the first verse of the third chapter of Genesis. It is *Nachash*. That is the name of the creature which beguiled Eve. The history of the creature is enclosed in the name, under cover of a bundle of ideas so incongruous and disconnected as not to be understood, until, in the revolutions of ages, sufficient knowledge of the thing named had been acquired by experience to furnish the key to unlock the book. We see around it the serpent, — the charmed, the enchanted, — watching closely, prying into designs, muttering and babbling without meaning, — hissing, whistling, deceitful, artful, — fetters, chains, — and a verb formed from the name, which signifies to be, or to become, *black*. *Any good overseer would recognize the negro's peculiarities in the definition of Nachash, and the verbs connected with it, if read to him from a Hebrew lexicon.*

" The Bible tells certain facts about negroes, which none but the best-informed planters and overseers know at the present day. The most learned divines are ignorant of them, not because they cannot read Hebrew, but because they cannot read Hebrew re-writ in the negro. Planters and overseers read it in the negroes; but they don't know that it is Hebrew, and that their evidence, if they could read Hebrew, would prove in any court of justice, to the satisfaction of any jury, that the writer of Genesis knew more about negroes than they did.

"The people of the United States followed Adam's example without knowing it, and got their slaves from the serpent-worshippers. The Seventy-two who translated the Bible into Greek rendered the word *Nachash* by *Ophiz*, 'a serpent.' There were so many meanings to the word, they were puzzled to tell which to choose. Dr. Clarke thought that ' orang-outang' would have been a better choice than ' serpent ' for the name of *a black creature, formed like a man*, with the gift of *speech* and *reason, a great deal of cunning, yet playful and good-natured, walking erect, a sorcerer*, and a slave to *something that charmed it. If the Seventy-two had lived in our day, they would have rendered the word Nachash, as the great Hebrew scholar of the East, but now of the West*, C. Blanchard Thompson, *has rendered it, by the word Negro.*

" The negroes brought from the Gold Coast into America, and their descendants, I studied in the cotton and cane-fields, in sickness and in health, under good masters and bad, and at the dissecting-table. What I thus learned in the book of Nature, I found, to my great surprise, had been revealed more than five thousand years previously in the Hebrew Bible. I discovered that they have no resentments for being flogged, as other people have; that liberty makes them miserable, instead of happy; that they submit themselves into slavery; are protected by a law of their nature, like mules, against being over-worked; that they were slaves by mind, or slaves by nature.

"Happily, as foretold, the seed of the woman is bruising the head of the serpent, and Christianity is setting the poor negro free from slavery to that evil spirit which seizes upon him whenever he gets beyond the hearing of the crack of the white man's whip."

When I had finished this remarkable article, — and I was so absorbed in its numerous details, that I quite forgot the cloud of mosquitos who spiked me in every accessible part of my body, and enjoyed, I doubt not, a rare banquet, — I fell at once under the conviction, that Samuel A. was a bit of a wag, — a man who could not keep the wit from bubbling up. I wanted to hear him preach: for I knew that he must be a terribly funny man; one, indeed, who would not dare to be as funny as he

THE NEGRO. 135

could, for fear of the most dreadful consequences, since men have been known to die of excessive laughter. He has done, I said, a very rich thing; for he has published, in a Review given to the most ultra proslavery doctrines, a paper which purports to be a balm for every tender conscience south of Mason and Dixon's line, while it is really a very neat piece of ridicule. Here is poison, labelled " Magnesia," for every diseased Southern stomach. The old gentleman is really swimming in the deepest waters of satire; and I fear, that, if these planters discover under what a great gull's wing they have taken shelter, Samuel A. will surely swing for it. When the proprietors of De Bow find out the joke, they will sprinkle their journal weekly with holy water, until a new volume sets in.

But, as I sat there wondering, — the merciless mosquitos, who had fed on me and were full, singing at the top of their voices, and calling in all their neighbors, — I began to feel, that, after all, it was not a joke. Samuel A. was really in earnest. His friends, perhaps, had been slightly troubled about the rights of slavery; and, to appease them, he had consented to take down his old Hebrew lexicon, and, with intellectual spade and pick, dig about the roots of Genesis a little. And there is no denying that he has done immense service to the cause. The rich planter is satisfied, that, the moment a man reads Hebrew, he is possessed with the desire to own slaves; and that all our abolition brethren of the North want is a sound lecture by some ripe Hebrew scholar, who shall read to them the first chapter of Genesis. If they can resist that, they are incorrigible.

I take to myself great credit for exhuming this document, which was dog-eared and dusty, and likely to pass into utter oblivion. It settles some questions of grave importance: —

First, The absolute necessity of having Hebrew taught in our public schools.

Second, That the slave-owner is entirely right when he counts his mules, niggers, and hogs, and says he has so many "head" in the aggregate; and our outcry against its inhumanity arises simply from the fact, that we are not acquainted with Holy Writ. Had we the desired knowledge, we should remember, that, in the twenty-fourth verse of the first chapter of Genesis, "the Lord said, Let the earth bring forth *naphesh chayah* (*alias* negroes), cattle, and creeping thing, and beast of the earth after his kind; and it was so." God puts negroes and cattles in the same catalogue; and if, after this, you are rash enough to reprove the slave-driver, you will quickly have your flank turned, and your centre thrown into disorder, by that sixty-four pounder, — the original Hebrew first chapter of Genesis.

Third, We learn the important fact, that, that, ethnologically, the negro precedes Adam. The said negro is simply a sort of preliminary step towards a white man: he is "a living creature with an immortal soul." After the earth had brought him forth, God said, "Now let us make something in our own image, and after our likeness;" and then Adam stepped into the garden of Eden, while the negro sat quietly under the branches of the tree in the centre of the garden, waiting for Eve.

Now, how unfortunate it is that the Seventy were so ignorant of Hebrew roots, or rather how unfortunate that Samuel A. was born two centuries too late! Had he been one of the Seventy, and that august body had hit upon the right word for *naphesh chayah*, and translated it "negro," what an infinite deal of trouble would have been saved! It would have been settled beyond all dispute, that the negro is nothing but a serpent, — a hissing, whistling, babbling, cunning creature; and all qualms about the slave-trade would have been appeased. England would have been saved a great deal of excitement and harsh feeling about the "middle passage;" and her money-bags would to-day be filled with the millions of dollars which her abolitionists

expended in freeing the black bondmen of the
West Indies. America would have had no war.
Instead of this feeling of chivalry and humaneness,
which is called abolitionism, the North and South
would be owners in the same slave-ships; and
there would be a generous rivalry as to which section of our loved land should import the greatest
number of blacks and make the largest fortunes.
Alas! the Seventy were ignorant of the infinite
injury they were doing to posterity, when they
slipped so easily by the real meaning of *naphesh
chayah*.

Possibly they were absorbed in a friendly game
of euchre at the critical moment; for I hear that
these old divines were given to some of the plea-
sures of a carnal world: and, if so, sure am I that
knaves were prominent cards. There is, however,
but one thing to do: appoint the Rev. Samuel A.
a committee to repair to the nearest place where a
medium can call up the recreant spirits of the
Seventy, and belabor them with a Hebrew lexicon.

I need not add, that, after sufficiently wondering
at this paper, my mind was tranquillized; and I
succeeded in my object, — which was to forget the
world, and dusty roads, and war, and my own weariness, in sleep. Only once was I disturbed in the
night. Just before dawn, my door opened, and an

odd "living creature with an immortal soul" entered my room. It was about the height of a man; and I doubted not, that, if Adam Clarke had been present, he would have at once pronounced it the veritable orang-outang, whose perfidious wiles were the destruction of Eve's innocence. I had just summoned courage to question it, and had indeed asked, "Who art thou that comest here?" and it had "babblingly, whistlingly" answered, "Ise de Naphesh chayah, de ophidian Bimana, who" — when the only remaining cock which the soldiers had left on the plantation crowed, and the spiritual Bimana beat a hasty retreat.

For four months my business brought me into constant contact with the negroes. I have seen them under nearly all circumstances: when they were listening to the twang of the banjo, and enjoying the luxury of a Saturday-afternoon dance; and when they have, glum, silent, sullen, just come from the whipping-house with their backs well scored. I have seen favorite house-servants, who were proud of their ability to read and write; and the old field-hands, who, trembling with age, fumbled their charms, and told me of the adventures and exploits of Lafitte. I have tried impartially to answer that question, which the North now puts to every man who has travelled in the South, "Are the blacks ready for freedom?" It may

be a question fraught with many a difficulty :
still I will say, that, for one, I am not afraid to
have the experiment tried. I am troubled about
no such results as are held up as bugbears in every
argument. The negroes are far more fit to be free
than many people who enjoy that inestimable privilege : they are fitter to be free than to be
slaves.

Of one thing I am sure : the slaves everywhere
have an *intense longing* to possess their own bodies,
and to govern their own fortunes. No one could
have accompanied our forces through the Têche
without being deeply impressed with this fact.
They crowded to the highway to see us pass ; and
clapped their hands, and sang and prayed, as banner after banner, beneath whose folds to-day there
are no slaves, went by. Their expressions are
quaint, but full of meaning. " Tank God ! de day is
come at last ! " said one old man, as he reverently
raised both hands in benediction over our boys. I
could not help feeling that there was no harm in
bowing my head, as the white-haired man hoped
God would take good care " of de young master."
Still I could not see the use of freedom to one so
aged ; and said, —

" Uncle, freedom will do you no good ; for you
are just on the edge of the grave."

" I knows dat, master ; I knows dat well enough:

but I've got my boys; and I bless you all, kase you give 'em free."

I rode on, wondering where that old man, who had been working in the field with a hoe or plough for fifty years, had got that longing, — if not from an instinct, which will hold the tiller when he is emancipated, and guide him safely towards civilization.

Such jubilee I never saw. The blacks took our sick into their little huts, and nursed them with all tenderness. Many a soldier will remember, how, when he fell out of the ranks during one of those severe marches, and the planter near by scowled and glowered so that he would not enter the rich man's door, some poor "aunty," black as the ace of spades, helped him to her own cabin, placed him on her own bed, made him tea and gruel, and nursed him as tenderly as his own sister would have done.

"Massa say dis bery mornin', 'De damn Yankees nebber get up to here!'" shouted another as we passed: "but I knowed better; we all knowed better dan dat. We'se been prayin' too long to de Lord to have him forgit us; and now you'se come, and we all free." On entering one plantation, a crowd of blacks surrounded us; and I wished that the stolid logicians, who prove by slate and pencil that the black has no parental regard, had been there. They pressed in crowds about us; and the first question was, " Young marster, now we'se free, can we go up to Massa Smith's plantation, and get our wives?" These questions were asked of us continually; and, when I told them that they might go, nothing could exceed their joy. One old man, when I gave him the required permission, turned away, saying, " Well, well, dese is blessed times shure!"

And so it was all along the road our army marched. It did not seem to be the spectacle, the display, they cared for: it was the one grand subject, which throbbed in every black breast from Brashear City to Alexandria. They stood at the gate with tubs of cold water; and they offered their shoes, their money, to the soldiers; and when you asked where their masters had hidden their horses, and whether there were any saddles, or anything that could be made available, in the stable, they told at once, if they knew. Once I said to a stalwart fellow, who looked as though he might know many a hiding-place, —

" Tom, you are trying to cheat me: you do know where I can get a horse; but you won't tell."

" Marster, 'fore God, I tells de truff. Ef I knowed, I'd tell shure. You give me free, and do you tink I wouldn't give you massa's horse, ef I knowed where he were?" And the little crowd all corroborated his testimony, and seemed hurt that I distrusted them.

Many a man who has boasted that all his slaves could be trusted, that he had often given his boy Jim hundreds of dollars to carry to the bank, and that not a hand on his plantation could be cajoled away, had his eyes opened wide on those days of our advance. Unwilling that either Confederate or Federal should confiscate his most valuable horses, he had very stealthily and carefully hidden them in the thick underbrush of the woods, a mile or a mile and a half away. Jim alone knew where they were. The Confederates came rushing by, and Jim stood with open mouth at the spectacle; and, when asked where his master's horses were, he, of course, stared in profound ignorance. When the Federal advance came along, a cavalry-man rode up on his jaded beast, and inquired, —

"Boys, can you tell me where I can get a fresh horse?"

And Jim was not at all bashful. He at once answered, —

"Yes, marster: I'll show you where de old man hid his stallion;" and forthwith trotted by the side of the cavalry-man until he exchanged his worn-out hack for a fine, sleek stallion worth a thousand dollars.

These instances were innumerable. I will venture to say, that nearly half our cavalry-horses were changed in the Têche country; and, in the vast majority of cases, it was the favorite servants who pointed out the hiding-place, and said, —

" You give us free, and we helps you all we can."

A curious instance of this kind came under my notice. Wheelock and I were riding along with the skirmishers towards Opelousas, on two beasts that were thoroughly jaded, when a black boy rushed out from a cabin in the most excited manner, and would hardly let our horses go by, crying out, —

" Master, if you wants me to, I will tell you where there is two splendid horses belonging to de ole man."

" How far off? " we asked.

" 'Bout half a mile, master; and hid in de thick cane-brake."

" But why, you young rascal, do you come here, and discover to us your master's property? You ought to have more love for him than to do such a thing."

The idea of love seemed to strike the boy as being very peculiar; and he only answered, —

" When my master begins to lub me, den it'll be time enough for me to lub him. What I wants is to get away. I want you to take me off from dis plantation, where I can be free."

It was not a particularly pleasant though a somewhat romantic thing to leave our columns, and go half a mile into the woods. The guerillas abounded ; and they had no scruples whatever about drawing a bead on a stray Union soldier.

Still we needed horses, and made the attempt. The beasts were not there. The black boy was confounded, but said he would call Jean.

Now, Jean was the only boy on the plantation who knew where those horses were. He was a favorite servant at the "big house;" and, when the owner discovered that the retreat of the horses was known to some of the hands, he told Jean to remove them secretly to some secure corner, where neither the hands whom he knew he could not trust nor the Federals could penetrate.

Jean was brought. He was forty-five years old, had a family, lived as well as a slave can live in the Têche country (which is one of the most cruel places in the State), and had received a great many favors from the "big house :" still he longed to be free. I said, —

"Jean, I hear you have hidden two good horses in the cane-brake. Will you show me where they are ?"

12

He hesitated a moment, as though revolving the subject in his mind, grew serious, and then said slowly and calmly, —

" Yes, master, I *will* show you where dem horses is. De ole fokes will kill me near-a-most, if dey ever finds it out; but you'se de people dat sets us free, and we poor colored fokes ought to do what little we can for you."

He led the way through fields half a mile, and then came to a very dense cane-brake. It was a ticklish place to be in ; but we were in such condition, that we were willing to run some risk. Jean disappeared, and soon brought out a fine gray American horse, as all horses foaled in the North are called; and then, disappearing a second time, came back bringing another. We mounted with all despatch, the black boy getting astride of a very lean beast he had managed to pick up, and hastened on for our advance.

Jean's is a sample of the kind of love the best negroes bear their masters. The more a slave knows, and the nearer he comes to being a self-supporting man, the less willing is he to live in servitude. With the first idea that enters a black man's head comes the desire for freedom. Keep him in the most brutal ignorance, and he expresses no particular desire to be free ; but teach him how to shoe a horse, let him learn the carpenter's trade, or allow him to attend you as your body-servant, and to hear the conversation of white folks, and he is ruined as a slave. You may allow him all the privileges which his position has a right to claim; you may give him presents, and try to endear him to you in all manner of ways, — still, in the great majority of cases, he chafes against the bars; and is not to be trusted for a moment, when it is possible to attain his freedom. There are, of course, exceptions to this rule. There are servants, generally female, who cannot be induced to leave the old home. They are sufficiently happy and contented as they are. They experience none of the horrors of slavery, and are attached to their master or mistress. Not so generally with the man. Somehow his brain is at work on the problem all the time. He may have every thing else, but still he is restless until he owns his body. Now, Jean was a good servant; one who daily came in contact with his owner. He visited other plantations, and saw and heard what no field-hand ever saw or heard. He was never whipped. But he had a wife and three little children; and he told me that he trembled lest some day he should go home, and find one of his little ones gone or his wife sold.

"For," said he, "these be hard times, and nobody knows whether they have much money at the big house or not."

Nevertheless, he told me he should stay on the plantation until he could get all his family away. He bade my black boy an affectionate farewell, gave him an extra shirt, and hoped that God would bless him.

As we rode by the crowd at the gate, some cried out, —

"Well, George, how is you?"

"All right now for de fust time in my life," he answered.

And he slapped the ribs of his poor old horse by bringing his bare legs against his side with prodigious force, and galloped off, singing, and in the merriest possible mood.

That boy I brought to New Orleans with me. He proved to be a fellow of pluck, and expressed a desire to go into the army. I had him enlisted as an engineer; and, when I was at Port Hudson, he found me out, and came rushing up to me to tell me what he had been doing. He will make a good soldier; and I congratulate myself on having taken a good hand from a secession cane-field, and placed him in the army of the Union.

But this instinctive love of and longing for freedom does not confine itself to words: it sometimes shows itself in lofty and heroic sufferings, willingly endured for its sake. We have been told so repeatedly of the dull, sluggish nature of the black man, and of the vast difference between him and the rude Saxon, that we have been led to believe there is no spirit, nothing indeed but a tame, insipid timidity, in the black's heart. A careful observer, on going through this State, would learn, that though, by the leaden weight of an irresistible and merciless public opinion, the majority of the slaves are kept in the most servile subjection, instances have constantly occurred of black men taking their lives in their hands, and risking every thing to be free. These instances of lofty heroism seldom get to the ears of the North. It would not be policy to have them rung out by the clarion eloquence of Phillips from the rostrums of New England. But go quietly to the hound-owner, who has a pack of a dozen or more full-blooded dogs, and ask him how much employment he has had in past years, and how many negroes his dogs have so torn that they died; or when you are riding with the planter, and you are both in a confidential mood, get him to tell you how in the floating prairie yonder, on a little mound of firm land, to which there is but a single narrow path over the tilting morass, a path known to very few, there have been from time to time little communities of negroes, six or a dozen or twenty, who have lived there for months. And they were the brightest hands on the place too. One day the overseer was testy, and struck them; and at once they boiled over at the indignity, very nearly killing the overseer, and then took to the swamps. Sometimes they come out at night, and the hands give them bacon and corn-meal. Again they come and steal a sheep: and somehow they manage to live there, and the planters can't get at them. It certainly required a brave and determined heart on the part of the negro to resist the popular feeling of all the planters of the State, and to defy the State laws, which winked at the overseer who shot a runaway slave dead, and to endure the privations of swamp-life, with a very dim prospect of ever getting to a free State, for the sake of his personal freedom. That negro certainly was something better than an " ophidian Bimana," and had an appreciation of the value of freedom that need not have shamed any Saxon in the land.

But, since the war commenced, brilliant examples of heroic endurance of suffering have transpired. I have listened to the adventures of one of these men, who was determined to be free at all hazards; and I have been thrilled with the interest of the narrative, and kindled with indignation against a white man who pretends to be a Christian, and who, with honeyed language, will tell you how he loves his hands, and how his people love him; but who, nevertheless, will set a dozen dogs on a black personification of a thousand dollars, if he chance to indulge a desire to be a man. It is at such times that one sees the peculiar beauties of this great missionary society, miscalled slavery; and it is at such times, too, that the chivalry of the Southern gentleman is exhibited to advantage. It is a picture, thank God, which stands in bold contrast against our American civilization; and is an anomaly, which, I hope, can have no existence after the war is over.

Immediately after Butler entered New Orleans, the slave-owners were compelled to keep a stricter vigilance over their hands. Fewer passes were given to slaves, allowing them to visit neighboring plantations; the lash was more freely used to intimidate, and keep the blacks in subjection; and fears of a general exodus were to such an extent entertained by the whites, that the civil police was largely increased, and all sorts of measures resorted to, to impress upon the negro's mind that he would be roughly used if ever he fell into the hands of the Yankees. This is the testimony of all with whom I have spoken. Indeed, the unanimity upon this point is quite remarkable. The master instinctively felt that he possessed only the hatred of his chattel, whose sympathy was given to the Union army. He knew that the negro was to be trusted only within good rifle-shot. Still, large numbers succeeded in escaping, and found refuge and freedom within the lines of the Federal force. I have talked with many who travelled from one to three hundred miles, encountering dangers enough to make a respectable novel, and who were prompted only by a desire to own their own bodies. The story they tell is quaint, but oftentimes thrilling. One which I recall, related by a lusty fellow of about four and twenty years, is so full of interest, that I must repeat it.

October was a slave, on a large cotton plantation in the southern part of Arkansas. When twenty years of age, he had married a yellow girl on the plantation, by whom he was blessed with one child. He said he had always been a restless hand, and entertained an instinctive hatred towards the overseer. He could never understand why that brutal man should stand over him with a whip, and, whenever he felt a little out of sorts, have the right to vent his spleen by a sharp cut over his (October's) shoulders. To be sure, the overseer was white, and he had been told that white people had received power from God " to do their will with the blacks ; " that these blacks were not regarded by God as good for much ; that some of them had souls, — those who worked faithfully ; and some were no better than the pigs that fed from the master's bounty. This, he said, he could never comprehend. He lay awake many a night, thinking of it. He talked the matter over with his wife; but neither of them could understand it. He only knew one thing, — that he hated the whole white race; and that, above all things else, he hated and cursed God. When he was well-nigh worn out by these thoughts, an old gray-headed preacher from the next plantation came into his cabin, and, being a very sympathetic man, got his whole story out of him. When he had told all, the old man hid his face in his hands, and murmured, "How long, O good Lord! how long?" Then, turning to October, he put his hand on his shoulder, and said impressively, " Octo, de white man is de liar, and de Lord tell de truff. We is a poor mis'able race; but God A'mighty love us just as much as he do de rich white fokes." " From that moment," said October, " I knowed what I wanted : it was to be free."

The next morning, with a lighter heart, he went into the field; and, when he came home at the accustomed hour for dinner, his wife and child were gone. There was the pork, all cut up, and ready to be fried; and down on the hearth, in the pan, was the corn-dough. No fire on the hearth; and, said he, " a feelin' to de room dat made me sit down in a chair, and cry like a baby."

Just then, the overseer appeared at the door.

"Where be my wife and my baby?" he cried frantically.

"What, October? Do you mean Mary and the pickaninny? Why, the old man was dunned most awfully this morning; and, knowing that you and your woman were a damned uneasy couple, he just slipped the other two away."

The nearest thing at hand was the iron pan, with the corn-dough in it. Quick as thought, October shied it at the overseer's head. It just missed him; but he saw at once that he had committed a crime which would be considered heinous by any slave jury. He then started for the swamp, while the enraged overseer went for his gun and dogs. He had no food, except three slices of pork which he had slipped into his pocket; and no clothing, except what he had on his back. He had a fearful task before him; but his agony fitted him for it. With wonderful speed, he rushed through the swamp till he came to a small bayou. This was fortunate; for the dogs would here lose his track. He swam across, and kept on the full run for half an hour; when the baying of the head hound proved that he was seen. On he went, and on the dog came. He had no weapon save a dull jack-knife, which he opened, and got ready for use. The head dog was on him; his sharp teeth were in his thigh; and the other dogs, four in all, were not far in the rear. With a great effort, he managed to get hold of the dog's throat with his left hand, and, with his right, brought down the old jack-knife blade just back of the skull of the hound. It was a lucky hit; for the dog let go his hold, and fell dead. He then limped on as fast as he could; and, coming across a thick club, he grasped it, resolving to die game. Two of the hounds were near enough to see him. There was no use in running: so he stopped to gather strength and get breath for the contest. The hounds rushed on furiously. One made his leap; when thwack came the cypress club on his head, and stunned him. The other dog fastened his teeth into the calf of his leg, and hung to him most savagely. He had lost his knife, and the club was of little use. He beat the brute as lustily as he could; but his blows did not drive him off. At last, he grew desperate. The overseer could not be far behind; and, if he came up, all was lost. He went down on his knees, and managed to get the hound by the throat. With both hands he clinched him, and at last had the satisfaction of seeing that the brute was choking. Still he held fast to his calf; and when he was choked dead, or rather senseless, so tenacious was the brute, that October was compelled to pull his jaws apart to get free. He then started on, limping badly.

Still his trials were but just begun. He had got rid of dogs; but now he was to encounter men who were just as merciless. He had no food; and his feet were sore, and badly cut. His clothes were torn nearly off his back; and as I think of the poor boy, worn with a heavy grief, without a friend in all the wide world, making his way through the dense jungle, and yet willingly enduring these things in the simple hope of being the possessor of his own body, and of getting to some place where no man would have the right to sell from his home those whom God had given him, I feel that there is something heroic and manly in him. He has proved his worthiness to enjoy that inalienable right which should be the birthright of all.

For ten days he wandered through the woods, travelling mostly by night; and at last, on a beautiful, bright morning, he came out in the road, and saw in the distance our flag floating in the breeze. "Then," said he, "I felt safe. I knew, dat, de moment I got close to dat flag-pole, I was free." And yet we have had generals in our army (God grant we have none now!) who would have forbidden that boy to come within our lines, and have delivered him over to his master, had that master come with his oily, lying lips, and stood upon his rights as a Southern gentleman. We are not worthy of those significant victories which follow on the heels of such a war as this; a war which is like a boiling caldron, in which right and wrong are simmering together, each boiling, bubbling, seething, to determine which shall become the precipitate, and which shall give character to the water which is to quench the thirst of the next generation; a war upon whose magnificent issues the old sages and heroes of the past are gazing from their homes in the great Hereafter with infinite solicitude, to assure themselves that we are worthy the mighty heritage of popular liberty which they bequeathed to us: I say, we are not yet ready for the end and the triumph, unless we forget the difference between the black and the white skin, and worship heroism and manliness wherever they may be found. Before that great day, — the day when the Almighty will give us back the old flag, torn, powder-stained, but glorious; the symbol of a people who are all free, — we must slough off this unmanly antipathy against those of darker hue; this corroding prejudice which holds us back from deeds of justice, and forces us into wronging four millions of American citizens, who will yet be found invaluable as agriculturists and soldiers, but whom we have delighted to sneer at as only niggers.

This story of October is not singular. I have met many men, in my travels through the department, whose experiences have been equally thrill-

ing.   There are scores of officers, whose body-
servants have endured all manner of trials in the
attempt to secure their freedom.   I have seen boys
with buckshot in their arms and in various parts
of their bodies, — the price they were willing to
pay to own themselves, and the last souvenir of
slavery.

So much I say to prove the universal longing, in
the negro's heart, after freedom.   I know there are
many in the North who believe that the black man
is in a kind of comatose state : he has worn the
chains so long, and has become so accustomed to
them, that he would feel at a loss without them.
Most planters will tell you that the slaves are the
most rollicking, and the least ambitious, people in
the world; if freedom were offered to them, they
are too well contented with their present careless
life to accept it; they can never be happy, except
as dependants of the whites.   But it is not so.
With the exception of a few favorite house-servants,
and a small number of people too old to take care
of themselves, all are wide awake, terribly so, on
this subject. · They have prayed about it, and met
in secret conclave to talk of it.

The planters little know how many times they
have been sleeping on a volcano.   While thinking
themselves secure from all harm, and believing that
their hands were in their cabins, dreaming, they

have been close to a bloody insurrection: the very thought of which the planter scouts, when talking to a Northerner; but which he has been in mortal dread of many and many a time. At midnight, the blacks have stolen from their plantations, and met in the cane-brake, or some other secure retreat, and talked of the Yankees, and prayed for them and for the flag of the free.

Again: the slaves of the South are not a happy people. No one can travel from plantation to plantation, from county to county, as I have done, without being strangely impressed with the universal gloom of the negro character. You may talk of the light-hearted, merry slave as much as you will: it is all rhetoric, and has no foundation whatever in fact. They are a sombre race, — a race who show that every effort has been made to crush them, — a race whose hearts have a chain and ball on them. Planters delight to tell you of the Saturday-afternoon dances, of the frolics when the day's work is over, and of the general hilarity which is noticed on a plantation. I have lived on plantations a week at a time; I have watched slaves under nearly all circumstances, — on the Saturday afternoon, in the evening, and at their balls: but I have been everywhere convinced that an unnatural gloom overspreads the negro's life. It is very seldom that you hear a good round laugh from a black man. He is timid and fearful, and seems like one walking in a dangerous place in the dark. But say, " Uncle, would you like to be free ? " and notice the twinkle in his eye as he looks at you searchingly, and, after concluding that you are his friend, says, with an ominous shake of the head, " Yes, master : all of us would *like* to be free ; but we don't see de way yet."

Still the serious question proposes itself here, Are these people fit to be free ? Can they, as a race, support themselves ? The answer, in my mind, is very clear. Why should they not be able, if there is work for them to do, to procure their three-quarters of a pound of pork and their half-dozen ears of corn per day ? Are they so foolish as to starve to death ? Look at this matter closely, and you will find the source of these assertions of the planter. He does not, for a moment, suppose that the black has not sense enough to procure his own subsistence. That is not his trouble. It is that the work on a sugar-plantation is, at certain times of the year, very trying; and he fears that the blacks, through what he calls their inevitable laziness, will prefer to live on their little patch of ground, rather than work for him, during the rolling season, for unreasonable wages. The planter is looking at his own interest simply, when he argues this point ; and, when he talks of the slave's laziness and imbe-

cility, he means, simply, that he will, through freedom, get beyond his reach, — nothing more. The
Southerner, in his heart, has not the least doubt
that the slave population have the ability to become a self-supporting people. Look down the
catalogue, and see for yourself how this is. In the
first place, we notice the house-servants, who are
cooks, chambermaids, body-servants : these can always find employment as well as white people of
the same class. Then come the hostlers, who are
generally very bright, and the gardeners, the black-
smiths, carpenters, and other hands, whose money
value is beyond the average. These, surely, can
find out the way to a subsistence ; for their trades
are always remunerative, and their services will
always be in demand. Next we come to the field-
hands ; and of these the brightest are generally the
ploughboys, some of them right smart and shrewd.
Then, lastly, we notice the clumsier sort, who, both
men and women, use the hoe and shovel. Who
of these are unable or unwilling to earn their five
pounds of pork (forty cents) and their hundred
ears of corn (a dollar) per week ? Just throw off
the yoke, and give them a fair trial. You would
soon find that they would become shrewd and
thrifty. Your big plantations would undoubtedly
suffer, and hence the sneers and opposition. It
would cost more to raise a crop of sugar ; for the

negro, no more willingly than the white man, will work night and day, for three months in the year, for poor clothing and wretched food. Louisiana, instead of consisting, for the most part, of thirteen hundred and fifty plantations, that cover from one to three and five thousand acres each, would be dotted all over with little homesteads of from two to a dozen, and from that to fifty acres each; while the population, in point of moral worth and vigor, would increase a thousand-fold, and the State at last become truly democratic and republican.

Another and a more important change would take place; this time, not so much in division of land, and extent of farming interest, as in the character of the citizens. There are geniuses among the blacks, men wonderfully gifted by nature. The race can give us minds whose thoughts we cannot afford to lose. Music, art, and science will spring into being with freedom. Four millions of people surely have some among them who are nobly gifted, and who only need to hear the chains drop to spring into a grander life. Now we get from them nothing but the play of their muscles; but let Freedom sing her song in the South, and these gifted sons, brightened by public schools, tamed by an outspoken, practical religion, and encouraged by an enlightened public opinion, will rise to the surface of society, worthy the companionship of aristocrat or *littérateur*.

I remember to have been called to Carrollton some time in February to inspect the condition of the negroes there. They had collected in very large numbers, from an area of country with a radius of forty miles, and formed themselves into colonies with from one to five hundred in each; and were living on three-quarters Government rations, and working in every way in which they could be made available. As soon as they were well settled, they built a rude church. The negro has a peculiarly emotional nature, and is very susceptible of a certain amount of religious influence. His religion is not always quite reasonable; it is a kind of nervous spasm, an uncontrollable ecstasy, with a great many: still it is the legitimate product of three generations of mental and physical depression.

I entered the low room devoted to church-purposes, bowing my head, not so much in reverence, I fear, as from the fact that my first act, after crawling through the door, was to add to my phrenological organs numerically by very close and sudden contact with the ceiling. It was a novel picture which presented itself. A full hundred blacks, of all shades, from the octoroon, generally pretty and pert, to the unmistakable Congo, were gathered together; and, for a few moments, perfect silence prevailed. No one seemed to dare to speak.

At length, however, a single voice, coming from a dark corner of the room, began a low, mournful chant, in which the whole assemblage joined by degrees. It was a strange song, with seemingly very little rhythm, and was what is termed in music a minor: it was not a psalm, nor a real song, as we understand these words; for there was nothing that approached the jubilant in it. It seemed more like a wail, a mournful, dirge-like expression of sorrow. At first, I was inclined to laugh, it was so far from what I had been accustomed to call music; then I felt uncomfortable, as though I could not endure it,. and half rose to leave the room; and at last, as the weird chorus rose a little above, and then fell a little below, the key-note, I was overcome by the real sadness and depression of soul which it seemed to symbolize. When it was ended, — and like our grandfathers, who indulged in unadulterated and unabridged " Watts " to the extent of fifteen or twenty verses, they sang for a full half-hour, — an old man knelt down to pray. His voice was at first low and indistinct: the prayer was purely an emotional effort. He seemed to gain impulse as he went on, and pretty soon burst out with an " O good, dear Lord! we pray for de cullered people. Thou knows well 'nuff what we'se been through : do, do, oh ! do, gib us free ! " when the whole audience swayed back and forward in their seats, and uttered in perfect harmony a sound like that caused by prolonging the letter " m " with the lips closed. One or two began this wild, mournful chorus ; and in an instant all joined in, and the sound swelled upwards and downwards like waves of the sea. It was a sort of universal amen to the words of him who prayed, and always commenced when the oppressions of the race were alluded to (as they always were in prayer), and when the preacher grew fervent (as he always did) while asking for all sorts of quaint blessings for the Union army.

At length, we were treated to the sermons. The first man who spoke was a downright, hard-thumping preacher. His object seemed to be to get himself into an ecstasy ; and, in the course of ten minutes, he accomplished his purpose. He lost all self-control ; and, intoning his remarks, took flights of rhetoric which would have made Whately dizzy, and produced logic which brought tears — of laughter — to my eyes. He was evidently a character, and produced some effect.

When he sat down, and the storm was over, a profound calm settled on the audience. For full five minutes, not a word was uttered. Then, from his quiet place in one corner, rose the man for whose sake I have made this digression, and introduced you to this strange negro-meeting. The moment I looked at him, I saw that he was no com-

mon man. He had a full forehead, a tall, commanding figure; and, as I afterwards ascertained, was a
confidential servant on one of the largest plantations in the State. There was no cant about him.
He was simply a genius, — gifted far beyond most
men, and needing only education to enable him to
take position among those who make rather than
follow public opinion. In his opening remarks, he
referred to a difficulty among the negroes who had
been led to expect pay for their work. I remember
his exact words. "My brethren," said he in the
most quiet and mellow tone, "I have been a slave
for six and thirty years; and, though I labored faithfully for my master, I never received at any one
time more than four bits; and if, as a slave, I
could work for my owner for six and thirty years,
now that I am a freeman, surely I can work for
Uncle Sam a little while, — just a little while, —
until he can find a fitting place for me, for nothing."
To the reader, it may be a common sentence; but
the effect was instantaneous. "Yes, yes," went
over the room: "if we're free, it's enough for
now." The question was settled with that audience, and better than I had done it with all my
arguments. Again he produced a queer, thrilling,
oratorical effect upon his hearers. "Brethren, I do
not care if *I* am a slave; I have reached maturity,
and can endure it: but" (and here his voice fell

almost to a whisper) " I have in yonder cabin a
child, a boy only five years of age, whom I love as
I do my life; and I thank God, I thank God, that I
am a freeman, *for his sake.*" Think of the kind of
people addressed, — unintelligent, rough, careless
field-hands ; and of him who, in that rudest of all
temples, spoke these lofty thoughts,— a man owned
by another, to whom Nature had given the genius
to see into and through the institution of slavery,
himself one of its victims, — and you will admit,
that the thought as well as the expression was
remarkable.

I remember, too, some of his phrases: they were
very beautiful, and were epic in grandeur. He
spoke of "*the rugged wood of the cross,*" whereto
the Saviour was nailed; and, after describing that
scene with as much power as I have ever known
an orator to exhibit, he reached the climax, when
he pictured the earthquake which rent the veil of
the temple, with this extremely beautiful expression: " And, my friends, *the earth was unable to endure the tremendous sacrilege, and trembled.*" He
held his rude audience with most perfect control;
subdued them, excited them, and, in fact, did what
he pleased with them. I recall one other expression, which struck me as being very effective. He
was beseeching his people to walk in the paths of
virtue ; and, when referring to the awful penalties

of disobedience, he said, " And, if you heed not the lessons of this dear Saviour, you will inevitably go to *that place which is filled with the unmixed wrath of Jehovah.*"

On coming out, I said, " This, of course, is a speech which he has committed to memory." But my friend assured me to the contrary. He said the man could talk as brilliantly at any time, and on any subject. Then my heart swelled against a system which keeps such a man in degradation, and has a well-regulated machinery which ruins the genius of a whole race. Commencing with the fatal presumption, — and an abominable insult to the Almighty it is, — that, collectively and individually, the blacks are imbeciles, these people have set to work, and formed an organization as complete as Masonry, within whose outer circle you and I can no more enter, being abolitionists, than we who are not masons can enter the door of a masonic lodge. The chief aim of the members of this organization being to make money; to establish an aristocracy and a wealthy landed gentry; and eventually, at some convenient time, to break the bond of union with the republican North, and invite some cast-off European prince to come and reign over them (for this latter purpose inheres in the heart of the organization), — they hope to base all this fine project upon the continued and sys-

tematic subjection of four millions of men, who
are as bright mentally, and brighter morally, and
as valuable by any measurement, as a large class
of poor whites, who, in the grand whirl of the vor-
tex, are kept just enough under the water to be
helpless, craven, cowardly, and half-drowned. By
this subjection, based on the falsest philosophy and
the greatest inhumanity, they have kept this whole
population on a dead level, and that level as far
beneath the position of a free white man as is possible. The clumsy, ungifted clod has been almost
equal to the bright and perhaps grandly gifted
genius. Slavery is the level; and the mean ones
have only sunk down to utter laziness and stupidity,
the sign of which has been corded into their bare
backs by a rawhide lash, which cuts to the blood
at every stroke ; and the lofty ones, — those richly
endowed by nature, — who, like the same class of
persons in the white race, needed only mental
training and discipline to develop minds that could
coin thoughts far above yours or mine, have risen
above this level only to the position of the hostler
or the body-servant, and then, in their ascent, have
invariably come to the end of their tether. Not
only has there been no vent practically (though I
have often heard the delicate theory of planters on
this subject, through which they have been enabled to rise by severing the tether, and reach the

14

manhood of freedom), but any incipient aspirations after a position higher than that which has been decreed their natural level by the fiat of their self-constituted judges has been effectually quenched, and driven back into the heart of the victim, as we drive canker back into the blood by alum, until, at last, it has well-nigh leavened the life of every vein and artery, and compelled the whole body to succumb to the mental and moral death of hopeless servitude.

Carlyle says that a man has a divine right to any position which he can possibly fill. If this is so, the culpability of those who will persist in refusing fair play in the general competition is beyond measure. They are no part of the real American people, either in sympathy or worthiness. They have no lot or part in the problem of political economy which history has thrust upon us, but are its sworn enemies. They are hostile to democracy in their politics, their social life and habits, and all their institutions. For the last half-century this has been ignored or denied, because the two sections of country have been woven together by the mighty web and woof of commercial interest; but, when the first gun was fired, the South took their proper position, — the position of traitors, — and publicly confessed that they had been plotting against the North and liberty for a whole generation.

Still, America is the great arena in which free government is to be tested. Not half of the continent, but the whole of it, God gave us in 1776; and as we would repel any foreign invader of our rights and our mission, so must we buckle on our armor against the foe in our midst. The war may last twenty years: still, if we yield, we fail, and must hereafter hide our heads in shame. It is not an optional matter with us. We cannot avoid the tremendous responsibility. The avalanche has started on its murderous path. If we have machinery to stop it, well; if not, we shall be crushed, and America is no more.

I have always heard a great deal about the patriarchal character of the planter. Indeed, in conversing with gentlemen who owned large estates, they have assured me in good faith, that the relation between their slaves and themselves was little short of parental. It is not only for the interest of the planter, it is also his duty, they say, to exercise a sort of providential vigilance over his hands. These beings are dependent upon him; and he is bound, by all the obligations of a man of honor and a Christian, to see that they are properly cared for.

I was charmed with this picture of the institution, and determined to look into the matter for myself. I found the description all rhetoric, as I expected. Why, only the small planters, those who own from ten to thirty hands, have any acquaint-. ance whatever with their people. I never yet have found a planter — and I have asked the question of two hundred — who could tell me the exact number of blacks on his estate, without referring to his books. The master knows, by personal observation, nothing of the way in which his slaves live. Once a day, perhaps, he rides on his fine horse over his grounds, and sees his hands at work in the distance. The overseer comes up on his Creole pony, and reports on the progress of the crop. This is all the contact between the planter and the great majority of his hands from one year to another. I went into a negro cabin on one of the finest estates on the river; and the old uncle told me he had been on the place twenty years, and his master had never entered his door. So much for the parental intimacy between the owner and the owned. The truth is, the negro and the mule are reckoned together. If both are tough and docile, it is well; if either is sick and dies, it is so much money out of pocket. That is all the master cares for his chattel.

The negro repays this galling indifference and this slavery by a quiet animosity against all white men. He always hates his overseer, and considers that he has done a good thing if he can disturb him in any way. He dares not show it openly, because the lash is the consequence; but once let him feel that he has the power, and he will show the planter what *he* thinks this much-boasted parental relation is worth. Already he begins to exhibit his indifference; and, in order to get the same amount of work out of him, the overseer, since the whip has been prohibited, is compelled to offer all kinds of small inducements. The moment he gets into a passion, and, forgetting that it is '63, and not '61, strikes the black man, down go the hoes and shovels of a dozen men, who stoutly protest against such treatment; while the victim marches off, spite of all entreaty, to the nearest provost-marshal, to enter a complaint. If these men are not ready to be freemen, they at least show their unfitness to be slaves. It is plain enough that they chafe, and long for something better.

Again: this love for their masters is shown by a couple of little incidents, for the truth of which I am able to vouch.

Mr. B——'s slaves all skedaddled last autumn, and came up to the city. After some time, and by a prudent expenditure among certain officers, most of them *were returned* to his plantation. One boy, however, was wanting. He was a valuable hand, because he was a carpenter, and young and tough. After searching all over the city for him in vain, he at last discovered that he had enlisted in one of the colored regiments, and was then in quarters at the Touro Buildings. He went there at once; and judge of his surprise, when, on entering the gate, he saw Joe in a soldier's suit, with an Enfield rifle in his hand, marching backwards and forwards, doing duty as guard! Now, had it been a white soldier, he would have politely lifted his hat, and asked permission to pass. This, of course, he could not do to a boy he had paid two thousand dollars for, and whom he had been accustomed to order about as he chose. Besides, Joe seemed to take no notice of him. Before this, if the boy met his master, he always lifted his hat; but now he marched back and forth as though unconscious that a Southern gentleman was near him, his fine, stalwart form shown off to great advantage by his soldier-clothes. After a moment's hesitation, Mr. B—— concluded to run guard. It was, however, a signal failure. The bayonet was in position in an instant, and in dangerous proximity to his body.

"Why, damn it, Joe! what are you doing?"

"Nobody can't pass, sir, widout a permit. Dose my orders, sir."

"But don't you know me, Joe? I have business with your colonel."

"Can't help it, sir,—must obey orders. Fall back, sir!"

Mr. B—— then tried to send a message to the colonel; but it was impossible. One negro would pretend to take it, and come back, saying the colonel would be at leisure in a few moments. After waiting a half-hour, another negro came down stairs with the message, that the colonel was engaged, and could not see anybody. Poor Mr. B—— pocketed the insult, saw he could make no headway, and went off cursing all negro regiments.

Those negroes were all runaway slaves. They had agreed that no white man should enter the gate, unless he had on a uniform. When one came, they did not "master" him: it was "sir." Oh, yes! they undoubtedly love their owners; and, when in their presence, will deliver their muskets up at once, knowing by the law of nature that they are the superior race!

Another gentleman found a favorite slave in the same regiment. In some way, he managed to elude the guard, and got into the building to search for his chattel. Pretty soon he heard a very suggestive whiz, and discovered to his surprise that a respectable cobble-stone had been on an excursion. Thinking nothing of it, he proceeded on his way; when another came whizzing by, this time altogether too close for comfort. He then discovered that he was himself the target, and that, by some good luck, the target had been missed twice. Not caring to test the accuracy of negro aim a third time, he began a masterly retreat. Before he got fairly out of the yard, however, he was the victim of a pretty serious joke. Little and big stones dropped close to him; all sorts of filth dropped on him; and he concluded that hunting up slaves who have got on the United-States uniform is not what some people may think it is. I could not help drawing another conclusion when I heard the story, for the victim told it to me himself; viz., that after all the superfluous rhetoric about the patriarchal institution, and the tender affection between owner and owned, there was another side to the story,— the side of fact, stern and inevitable, which shows us the slave hating his master, and wanting only the opportunity and the power to show it.

The question has been asked, Will the negroes fight ? Wiseacres, generally negrophobes, and members of the copperhead order of politicians, have shaken their heads, and deduced all sorts of *à priori* arguments to prove that they are all cowards. Their *confrères* in the South have laughed the scheme to scorn, and told us that the negro does not know which end of the rifle is the but, and which the muzzle; and that he always trembles when a gun is fired. So weighty has been the logic used, that the people have kept very quiet on the subject; feeling that it is like thin ice, a little dangerous for a man who wants to keep his head above water, and that it is best to leave it to take care of itself. Only a few fanatics, who never take a practical view of any subject, have sworn that the blacks will fight as well as white men; but their voices have not been heeded. This coma of the people, at last, or rather at first, found its way into the White House; and he, the honest President, who always wants the dear people to instruct him how to act, concluded that a kind Providence would make the suggestion when it was time to act, and so did nothing. A few black soldiers were enlisted by Gen. Sherman, who received very vague orders to make such use of negroes as he saw fit; though he was given to understand, that he was not to arm them generally. These troops very soon learned which was the but, and which the muzzle, of the rifle; and dressed into as straight a line, and went through the manual as accurately, as their white brethren. Still no impression was made on the people. Then Higginson, with his regiment, committed all sorts of depredations on the rebels; went out on daring reconnoissances, had pitched battles with the enemy, and did not show the white feather. He says, "The blacks are brave, true, soldierly, and unconditionally loyal."

15

Then there have been numberless instances of personal daring and heroism which ought not to be forgotten. I have a servant (Tom Taylor), black and shiny as patent-leather, who was present at the battle of Baton Rouge, and behaved splendidly. He was the only man on the field with an ambulance. He caught a runaway horse and buggy, and drove where the fight was thickest; and, when a soldier fell, he took him in his arms, placed him in his buggy, and drove him to the hospital. This he continued to do while the fight lasted. Gen. Dudley spoke in the highest terms of his bravery, and said he did good service on that bloody day.

He came to me one morning in great heat, and trembling violently.

"Why, Tom, what's the matter?"

"O lieutenant! my old master's down below, an' I 'spec' he wants me. Now, I tell you what: if a white man acts gallantly on de field, and gives ebbery ting he got for his country, de people all praise him; but, if a black man does the same ting, nobody cares a cent. Now, I did all I could at Baton Rouge; and what I ought to have is my freedom."

"And that, Tom, you shall have. If your master comes to get you, I will most assuredly shoot him."

He did not fear rebel bullets; but at thought of his master, and a return to slavery, his joints gave way, and he muttered and stuttered so that I could hardly understand him.

He was in high spirits the next day, as cheery as a cricket, and made a characteristic speech: "Lieutenant," he said, "de ole flag neber did wave quite right. There was something wrong about it, — there wasn't any star in it for the black man. Perhaps there was in those you made in de North; but, when they got down here, the sun was so hot, we couldn't see it. But, since the war, it's all right. The black man has his star: *it is the big one in the middle.*" Tom is a rough boy; but, unconsciously, he once in a while stumbles upon a huge fact.

Gen. Butler told the truth when he said it was because the negro was a fighter that he was captured, and sold into slavery. Had he been a stick, he would have skulked behind a tree at that particular time, and would now be quietly eating his tropical mush under the shade of a banana-tree in the Guinea Coast.

It is not necessary to refer to historical instances of the daring of the blacks; to tell over again how they fought under Toussaint L'Overture, until the tried troops of Napoleon stood still in astonishment, and then beat a hasty retreat: nor is it necessary to speak of those forces which have always formed

a part of every European *corps d'armée.* These
facts are all familiar, and even trite ; and they seem
to produce no influence whatever.   Either our prejudice or our ignorance is so mighty, that we have
predetermined not to give the negroes the benefit
of the doubt, and try them.   " Give them guns, put
them into the field, and bring them up into line of
battle in front of those who have been in the habit
of commanding them,—the true Southern gentlemen, — and they will throw away their arms, and
flee in terror like so many monkeys."   That is
what we are told ; and we more than half believe it.

Mr. J. B. Jones has published what he thinks —
and he is entirely correct in his estimate — is a
remarkable book.   It was written some years ago,
and pretends to give a transcript of some of the
scenes which would occur if a civil war should
ever come upon us.   Among other subjects, he, of
course, has something to say of the negro, — not in
his capacity as a field or a house servant, but as a
soldier enlisted by the fanatic North.   I will give
his own words, sure that they will explain themselves : —

" Every disposition had been made for a decisive
battle the following day ; and most of the officers
retired early to their couches in quest of repose.
Gen. Toler alone was wakeful, and strode to and

fro in his tent. On turning once, he saw the canvas slightly agitated. He paused, and gazed steadily; and, a moment after, the following words reached his ear : —

"Massa John ! Massa John ! "

"Who's there ? " demanded the general.

"It's me, Massa John."

"And who the devil's me ? Let me see your face."

"Don't you know me, Massa John ? " asked a very black negro, creeping under the canvas, and rising in front of the astonished general.

"If it were not for the red flannel on your collar, and epaulet on your shoulder, with bright buttons and sword, I should say you were my slave Scipio."

"Dat's it, dat's it, Massa John ! " said the negro. "I am so still, dough dey call me Capt. Scip. I been belonging to de grand army under Gen. Fell."

"And now you have deserted to your master, Scip ? "

"Not dzactly dat, Massa John : *but d—n if I fight*, Massa John ; and dat's de way all de niggers is thinking and talking too ! "

"Ha ! is that so, Scipio ? " asked the general quickly, at the same time advancing, and grasping the hand of his faithful slave.

"It's just so, Massa John ! " replied Scipio, while

great tears ran down his cheeks. "You know you learnt me to read, Massa John? Well, I got one of de plocklamations of Gen. Ruffleton," — a supposed rebel general, in whom the negro confides naturally, — "which says we'se all to be slaves in de North as well as in de South. I had it and kep it for more dan a week, and read it every night by de pine knots to de colored captains, till I got through wid em all."

"You did, Scipio?"

"Sartain, Massa John! De niggers ain't 'lowed to be higher dan captain. But all de captains is been splanin de plocklamation to de men; and now we'se all ready."

"Ready for what, Scipio?"

"To break up and go home, Massa John, and 'tend to our work among our wifes and children."

"Is that so, Scipio? Why, it is understood Fell intends to lead you into battle to-morrow."

"I know dat, Massa John! We said he must let us fight, or we'd desart. I put 'em all up to dat, Massa John; and now all's 'ranged. To-morrow, all you'll have to do will be to jus gallop your white horse right up to us, and order us to throw down our arms, and go about our business. Dat's all!"

"Scipio, I know you love me. We were boys together, almost like brothers" (and, indeed, the slave in the South is more like a member of his

master's family than the free negro of the North is
like a freeman). " Scipio, I shall trust you. If you
deceive me, I shall perish, and my death will weigh
upon your conscience."

" Stop, Massa John; you're breaking my heart!"
exclaimed Scipio, prostrating himself, and embra-
cing his master's knees. " But if Scipio's 'ceiving
Massa John, dat he loves so much, may he roast in
brimstone fires for eber and eber! "

" I will trust you, Scipio. You will know me
by my white horse, which you trained from a colt;
and I am sure he would know you, if it were not
for your military trappings. When you see me
approach, contrive to be near the spot where I
shall address the men."

" I'll be dar, Massa John, — never fear! And
all de captains and all de men will know what's to
be done. I've been preparing 'em! Dey all understand. De white horse'll be looked for. Ride
right up to us. Nebber mind what the white
soldiers say; dey'll think you're desartin."

" Scipio, your hand! If this scheme of yours
succeeds " —

" Now, don't say so, Massa John; don't say I
shall have my freedom. I want to be wid you all
your life; and I won't be free, no how you can fix
it."

" Then farewell, Scipio, till to-morrow! "

"A moment after, Scipio disappeared; and the general resumed his promenade, resolved to hazard every thing on the fidelity of his slave.

"Early in the morning, Gen. Fell put his army in motion, and Gen. Toler awaited his approach behind the breastworks which had been constructed the day before. Not a shot was fired, except at the extreme left, where the white soldiers engaged; and these formed but an inconsiderable portion of Fell's army. On the black mass advanced, maintaining an ominous silence. The white officers were in the rear, urging the slaves before them; while Fell himself looked on in amazement from a neighboring hill. No smoke arose from the plain; no reports of fire-arms were heard, save from the most distant part of the field.

"It was then that Gen. Toler, in despite of remonstrances, galloped towards the interminable array of slaves; nor did he pause until he was within a few paces of the foremost ranks, and not a shot had been fired at him.

"What are you doing here?" he exclaimed in a loud voice. "Why are you in arms against your masters? I tell you, the Northern abolitionists have deceived you. They are determined to be your masters themselves; and you all know what hard masters the Yankees make. Throw down your arms, and go home, and I will forgive you. Go, I say!"

" Then Scipio rushed out of the ranks, and gave the preconcerted signal; and the sky was rent with cheers for Gen. Toler and the South.

" They threw down their arms; but, a moment after, snatched them up again, and demanded to be led against Fell, who had deceived them."

This certainly is a remarkable piece of light literature. Mr. Jones is a *confrère* of the Rev. Samuel A., or rather his competitor; for the struggle with both is to tell a lie so huge, that it shall look like the truth. This writer of light literature knew perfectly well, that a Northerner — at least one who was likely to see disagreeable things — was effectually tabooed all tours of investigation or pleasure south of Washington by the prospect of tar and other unpleasant and odorous appliances, with which the chivalry have been in the habit of treating every honest man; and, standing within the charmed circle himself (he is probably a Yankee, who has married a plantation), he is desirous of instructing the outside barbarians how they treat the animals in the menagerie, and so tells us what we are told by all other planters, — that the owner makes every possible effort to be a father to all on his estate; and I am willing to take his own testimony, and admit, that his labor in this direction is excessive, and that, to a greater or less extent, he succeeds.

> " Who does the best his circumstance allows,
>   Does well, acts nobly: angels could no more."

I feel sure that the whole community of Southern gentlemen were delighted with this publication. They laughed in their sleeves as lie after lie rolled up on each successive page, and wondered if there was even a Northern man with Southern feelings who would be deceived by it. Nevertheless, they subscribed largely to " secretly circulate" this " political and inflammatory document " among the unenlightened heathen of the North. Ah! Mr. Cartwright, you sold all *your* honesty and manhood to a wealthy parish; and poor, dear Mr. Jones, you filled your pockets with silver. You have both done very well in this world; for your strategy has been masterly. But I fear there is not a sensible school-boy who is not able to give the exact latitude and longitude of your geographical position in the hereafter: if you prefer Dante, it will be at the pole; and, if you have an affection for Milton, it will be in the tropics.

I said to a huge negro the other day, —

" Tom, they tell me that you won't fight if you do enlist; and that you love your masters so much, that, the moment you meet them on the battle-field, you will throw down your own arms, and rush into theirs. Is that so ? "

He was leaning against a gate-post, with his

arms folded; but he straightened up at my question, and his dull eye flashed as he replied, —

"Lieutenant, I know dey says dese tings; but dey lies. Our masters may talk now all dey choose; but one ting's sartin, — *dey don't dare to try us.* Jess put de guns into our hans, and you'll soon see dat we not only knows *how* to shoot, but *who* to shoot. *My* master wouldn't be wuff much ef I was a soldier."

This little speech of Tom's is the solid, homely truth of the matter. It is impossible for me to use such forcible or expressive language ; but it is just what I have meant in the last dozen pages.

Now for the great fact of the matter, — the fact of the war, which dashes all theories of Southerners and copperheads with tears. The bubble has been shivered into a thousand atoms, like a Prince Rupert's glass, by the storming of Port Hudson. The pluck of the negro as a soldier was fairly tried there in one of the hottest charges of the war. There were two regiments of Louisiana negroes in the right wing of the attacking force. Nobody trusted them. The West-Point generals shirked the responsibility of having them in their brigades. They were nothing but "nigger regiments," — the exponents of a pet idea of certain crazy people in the North. The Southerners joined in the chorus of croakers, and sneered, and intimated that things

were come to a pretty pass when we put guns into
the hands of men who were as likely to shoot themselves as any one else, and drew them up in line
against the chivalry of the South; and so the whole
current of popular feeling was against them.   Still
they drilled well; yes, they dressed into line mag-
nificently, — a stalwart, heavy-chested set of fellows! They handled their muskets, too, in very
soldierly fashion; but it was only by resolutely
stemming the tide, by the most independent persistence, that the regiments kept their position.
When first formed, they were laid on the shelf.
They camped in the mud in Algiers or Baton
Rouge eighteen months, rubbing their gun-barrels.
At last came the siege of Port Hudson.   Every
man was needed; and, more and better, Banks had
no prejudice against color.   In spite of some opposition, they were put into the field by the side of
white soldiers.   They were quiet, remaining within
their camp-lines, holding their little meetings,
hardly ever riotous, seldom drunk, never trespass-
ing beyond their lines; and their presence was
soon forgotten.

In good time, the morning came when the first
assault was made.   The distance between the camp
of the assaulting party and the works of the enemy
was a half-mile, more or less.   The ground was
ragged and broken, full of gullies, and strewn with

timber placed there by the rebels to obstruct our progress. When our forces got near enough to the fortifications, they had to sustain, besides the direct fire upon their front, a severe enfilading fire from some heavy guns. Altogether, it was an assault that required men of the utmost daring and pluck.

The charge was ordered. The negro regiments advanced, and very soon came into the grape of the foe. They had never smelt powder before; but (their officers say) there was an eagerness, a wild, uncontrollable enthusiasm, about them, which was quite wonderful. They charged directly in the face of the storm of bullets, square up to the ditch, which is on this side the earth-works, and six feet deep and twenty feet wide. They were most horridly cut up; yet they retired in good order, and, when called again into line, answered at once. A second time, on the double-quick, they rushed up to the ditch, and again fell back. They were dressed into line a third time, and advanced. "When within a few rods of the enemy's works," said one of their officers, "they became perfectly uncontrollable. We could not keep up with them. Their eagerness never was matched. Instead of cowardice, they seemed to have no conception of fear. The ditch troubled them. The enemy, their masters, whom they love so dearly, were beyond; and they chafed beyond measure. Just

then, the two regiments set up a yell. They were
close to the foe. It was a sound unlike any thing
I ever heard, — a wild, unearthly noise. It came
across me at the time, that it *was the slavery of a
thousand years finding vent.*"

The vexed question is settled for ever, thank
God! The commanding general, in his official report, speaks in the most complimentary way of
their behavior. They have fairly won a name, and
won it by undoubted bravery. If, after this, we
talk of negro regiments sneeringly, we are to be
pitied for our littleness, and despised for our ignorance. The only difficulty to be found with
them is one not often complained of. It is, that
they are apt to go too far. They become passion-
ate, fearfully excited, and their officers lose control
of them. In battle they are not merciful. So complete is their hatred of the rebels, that they want
to exterminate them. It would hardly do to put
a copperhead general over a brigade of negroes;
one, for instance, like that worthy of the Potomac
army, who disgraced a lieutenant the other day
for taking a chicken from a secessionist, and who
wants to fight in such way, that, if any blood is
spilled, it shall be our boys who bleed, and not
the traitors. He would be most horridly shocked
to see the way in which the negroes go into
battle; and would surely predict, alas! that the

end of the war was close at hand. One thing is
certain: it will be a most unfortunate thing for
our "erring Southern brethren" when we con-
clude to do what we ought to have had sense
enough to do a year and a half ago, — recruit all
the able-bodied blacks on the plantations, in every
Southern department, and then send our own boys
home to keep up the arts of peace, and do such a
thriving business that we shall not feel the weight
of the war-tax. That can be done; and, when it
is done, we shall have one of the most terrible
forces of fighting material the world ever saw. I
do not know that it would be terrible in Mexico or
Europe, or against any other foe. But I am will-
ling to aver, after a nine-months' intimate acquaint-
ance with thousands of negroes, that, between them
and the whites of the South, there exists a most
deadly hostility. It is the natural result of years
of slavery. Let the planter talk as he pleases
about cowardice, ignorance, and love of the master.
Put a good gun into his slave's hands, let him know
that he will be protected, and you may stake your
life that he will make a bee-line for his master's
house, with bayonet fixed; and, when he comes
out of the door again, *the same man does not own
him.*

One of the brightest boys now before Port Hudson I brought from a plantation in the Têche, and

put into the army. He is as tough as a pine-knot;
has lived out of doors all his life; is not afraid of
chills and fever; has never been attacked with
that formidable climatic disease called *debilitas*,
for which there is no remedy, but which yet is
actually so decimating our army, that, one day, two
regiments reported for duty, respectively, ninety
men and sixty men. He was sitting in my room
one day, talking of the army.

"Lieutenant, why don't the Union people *kill*
more? What for dey take any prisoners? Why
don't dey sweep 'em, like as with a broom? then
we'll be all right, and can commence all over
again."

"Because, George, that would not be right."

"What! not right to kill your enemies? I tell
you what, — we black people won't be troubled
much in that way."

"Why, you would not kill, when there is no
need; would you?"

"But there is need. The Bible says, sweep 'em
with a besom. Clear the country. There is no
good in any of them. You'se too merciful!"

"Not more merciful, George, than we ought to
be. I fear you hate all the Southerners."

"Of course I do!" And he turned round in his
chair, as though surprised that I thought he could
do any thing else. "Kill 'em all! that is my
motto."

"George, you should hate nobody," I said, very tamely indeed; for I knew the fellow was more than half right.

"O lieutenant! it's very well for you to talk; *you can afford to: you haven't got any thing partic-'lar against them fokes. Your back ain't cut up as mine is. You ain't heard screamin' wimmin, and seen the blood run at every lick, just 'cause a woman wouldn't leave her husband and sleep with the over-seer. They never done you such things; but I could kill 'em easy, — children, wimmin, and all.*"

This is a fair exhibition of the real feeling be-tween the slave and the white man.

There is no reasonable doubt, that the negro can be made to carry on this war. He is providentially placed in our way for this very purpose. Matters have so arranged themselves, that he can be the means, after we have tardily and half mistrustfully told him he is free, of bringing out of the blood and slaughter of these years the new Union; when the country shall be so equalized, that the New-Englander can go to Charleston, and say what he pleases with impunity; and when, instead of sneer-ing at our free schools, the Southerners will dot the hillsides and plains of the South with the little red ochre roofs, beneath which the history of true republicanism must always be written. God grant that we may not blunder in this thing! We need our boys at home, and we can have them here as well as not. We need the negro in the field; and, ever since the war broke out, he has been beseeching, as a privilege, that he might fight for his country. Down with all prejudice! it has kept us back long enough. Do justice to others, and then we shall begin to see the end, the glorious end, where is victory, peace, prosperity, and a better Union than we have ever had.

CHAPTER V.

CHARACTERS.

I THINK it is very generally conceded that war is not only a terrible evil, but also a terrible necessity. To be sure, the race has reached such a point of culture, that the love of mere military fame has well-nigh departed from our history, and there is not the same satisfaction which the heroes of the olden time seemed to feel in a continuous career of bloodshed, daring exploits, and narrow escapes. We enter upon a war only as a last resort, and then with the greatest reluctance. Still, in our own short history, reaching back some two centuries, we have had four wars, which were felt in the very heart of the nation. Almost every generation passes through an experience of this kind. When I was younger, and eager that the millennium should be reached at once, I felt that every century decreased the number of wars; but I now find that the chief difference between the nineteenth century and its predecessors lies in the patent fact, that our contests are sharper, and more quickly over. This is due to the murderous character of the machinery used.　Years ago, two armies might have a pitched battle, and struggle from sunrise to sunset, leaving on the field no more than we now leave after a hot fight of a couple of hours.

Nor do I see so much likelihood that the time will ever come, when human passions, and royal and pedagogical and popular caprice, shall be so subdued, and human interests so directed, that the resort to arms will not be thought of.　Our progress in this matter has been so slow, and war seems to occupy so prominent and important a position in history, that I find my time better employed in discovering the uses of war, than in seeking evidence of its very general decrease.　These " offences " must come : it is in the nature of things that they shall.　Under the overruling Providence, the crushing, social avalanche, leaving death and desolation in its track, undoubtedly has its mission, and accomplishes some great good.　" But woe unto that man by whom they come ! "

I know the terrible war-storm is horrible.　Thousands of homes are in tears : mothers and fathers are praying that their households may escape the fiery death-shaft.　The eyes ache as they look on the vast ruin, and the heart aches as it recognizes the necessity of such wild sorrow.　Society is roughly purged of its evils ; but when the storm is over, and the thundering of artillery has ceased, we find that our world is, after all, a better world. It is terrible treatment; but it cures us of all our ills. See if it is not so.

First, Society, which was, through a long peace, sluggish, careless, and dulled by long prosperity, is roused, awakened, and completely thrown out of its old life into a new one. New powers are developed, and a better knowledge of itself is gained. It learns to estimate its blessings more justly, and to recognize its duties more acutely.

Secondly, The men who controlled society, and who had begun to be old, conservative, and rusty, being unable to meet the great emergency, are all swept away; and the tremendous convulsion gives birth to a new set of men; men with fresher minds and impulses; men eager, because they have young blood in them, to grapple with the new difficulties of the new life.

It is in this way that society has always been remodelled. In a long peace, men shrink up, and become selfish. Every thing, even literature and religion, grows stale and musty. Nobleness narrows to meanness; chivalry, to cowardice; and the greatest and best aims of life are lost in selfishness. Iron-handed war is our great physician.

I am particularly interested in some of the scenes which occur while the convulsion is taking

place. How beautifully human nature uncovers
itself, and displays all its fair proportions and all
its ugliness! The inmost depths of the soul are
opened to view. Elements of character, which in
peace were latent, rise at once to the surface. In
a week, ay, in a day, men change their estimates
of themselves, and we change our valuation of
them. The old scales and the old rule are thrown
out of doors upon the heap of rubbish; for the
mere feet and inches high of one's social position,
and the pounds and ounces of his fortune, no longer
make a man great or little in our estimation. For
the nonce, intrinsic worth alone brings honor
and the love of the people. The showy shams,
who have gilded themselves all over, and, by a
peculiar genius for wriggling, have worked their
way up so high that their folly is all the more conspicuous, come tumbling down to the ground with
a crash; while the modest youth, whose only care
has been not to attract attention, is pushed, by the
actual force of his own merit, into the admiration
of society. After a six-months' campaign, the
little ones, whether they have shoulder-straps or
not, are known and trusted for just what they are,
and not one iota more; and the brave ones, privates and officers, rise to the proper level in the
estimation of the regiment, which is a community
whose public opinion is omnipotent.

When the war first broke out, it was proposed in town-meeting, that a regiment be gathered from the young men of the county, and their services tendered to the Government. Old Mr. Bagg, whose blood runs sluggishly enough now, and who, of course, does not appreciate this generous outgush of enthusiasm, opposed the motion. He did not believe in war; first, because he was old, was working his way along quietly towards the grave, and did not want to be disturbed by torch-light processions, fiery speeches, and flaming articles in the " County Gazette." He is not to blame for all this. It is one of the legitimate consequences of growing old. Forty years ago, he would have applied at once for a commission, and gone to the field with a wildly beating, eager heart; but forty years have had their influence, and now he believes in peace at any cost. Second, he did not believe in war, — though he does not state this in his speech, — because he is doing a large business, which will be seriously affected by the loss of the Southern trade. If you should tell him that this was one reason why he was a peace-man, he would probably feel insulted; for it may be that he is not aware of it himself, so subtly do a man's interests influence his opinions. At any rate, he uses strong language at the town-meeting, is hissed by the young men, grows red and very indignant; and, from the moment he sits down, he firmly believes that the nation is insanely running its head against the wall, and that the new generation, who are taking matters into their own hands, have sadly degenerated from the standard of their fathers. He is supported in his position by a dozen or a score of white-headed men, who have not been able to keep up with the times; and by a dozen young men, whose conservatism indicates the presence of some physical disease, and who should at once be confined to the hospital, and dosed until their blood runs faster. These men form a clique; and, while the war lasts, they will stand aloof, and grumble. Every defeat they will chuckle over, and every victory they will sneer at. They are a constant irritation, and a perpetual nuisance: still, the best way is to let them talk freely, and make no reply. Pray, don't fall into error, and convene an indignation meeting, and vote to ride them on a rail. This will never do. You are five hundred, and they are fifty; and I remember the impulsive generosity in the great public heart. If you proceed to extremes, you will only make them conspicuous, and excite pity for them, and convert them into martyrs; in which case, the chances are that they will run for one of the town-offices the next year, and get into a place where they can do you harm. Let them alone, and they will die a natural death.

By an overwhelming majority, it is voted to raise the regiment; and, in thirty days, the thing is done. But matters do not run quite smoothly. The colonel is just the man to command a large body of soldiers. He has a splendid figure, looks like a brigadier in his uniform, and made a thousand rousing speeches, that caused all the youths to shout, and all the young girls to clap their little gloved hands with delight. He will, undoubtedly, do himself and the country great credit. The lieutenant-colonel — Heaven only knows how he got his commission — is quiet, modest Mr. Tagg, who never went to parties, but was always moping over his books, — the very last man who should go into the field. A great many wise men shake their heads, and feel that he is one of the unfortunate appointments. Then there is Capt. Blunt, who has always had a reputation for courage, and who has told large stories of his brave deeds in the woods, among the wolves and panthers. When he gets hold of the rebels, there will be warm work. He will come home all covered with blood, powder-stains, and glory. But there is Capt. Rack, of whom little is expected. He was the village dandy. He always wore spotless linen and gloves. His hair was never out of order, and his handkerchief was always redolent of some sweet perfume. How the young ladies can spare him, no one knows; and how he can deprive himself of their society, is an equal mystery. But there he stands, fearfully tidy, in front of his company; while the old men look at him with a kind of disgust, and bet that he will fall to the rear when the first musket is fired.

And so, throughout the regiment, the officers have all been gained by the usual amount of wire-pulling, and proper and prudent expenditure of small and large sums of money. The villagers have formed their opinion of each, and feel sure that the said opinion is correct. A thousand untried men, who are to enter a new field, to walk through a fiery furnace which will surely try the inmost soul of each, stand there, dressed into line, with bright buttons, muskets, and swords; while maidens, mothers, fathers, and wives look on with mingled pride and sadness.

At length, they are in the field. There are no tents now, and only hard-tack and coffee for food. They are to sleep under the trees or in the bushes; and, to-morrow, they are to charge the enemy's works. Those works are on the other edge of the plain, right ahead of them; and, every once in a while, a quart of grape comes whistling through the woods, and more than once the sharpshooters have picked off a man. They have been in the service six months; but they have never smelt powder before.

The next morning comes; and, with three other regiments, they are formed into line of battle, and commence the approach. The fire in the furnace is growing hot now. It is impossible to avoid the ordeal. What is in the men's souls will certainly be forced out. The enemy says nothing; for he has no powder to lose. You will hear from him soon. On they march, — tramp, tramp, tramp; and when within fifty rods, just as the order to double-quick is given, whiz, whiz, come the leaden ounces, and rut, rut, comes the grape by the half-bushel. A dozen, twenty, fifty, ay, a hundred, fall. Now, then, where's that colonel who looked so like a briga-dier? You may look twice, and not find him. He has been having symptoms of the colic for the last three days, and this morning it came on with tre-mendous force. You will find him on his back, under a tree, just out of range of the enemy's guns; and, until he sees you, he is very quiet. But such is the nature of his disease, that, the moment you approach, he applies both hands to the stomachic regions, and utters such piteous groans, that, unless you are an old soldier, you will proba-bly waste a half-hour sitting by his side and com-forting him. He groans out in intervals, "It's too

bad — just as we were — going to have a fight ! If
I was only " — (here a double-headed groan) —
" well — I would like to make these fellows — feel
my sword."

Well, where is modest Mr. Tagg? He is not a
man of words ; but the boys all like him. He has
been kind, strict, and considerate, and has done
all he could for the command. You will find him
at the head of his regiment ; and when the line
breaks, because the balls come like a shower, he
quietly walks along its whole length, saying a few
kind words, which thrill his men, and compel them
to follow wherever he will lead. His quick eye
notes at once the absentees. Away back there,
he sees Capt. Blunt, who has fought so many
panthers, lying snugly on the ground, determined
not to be killed this time, and complaining of a
sun-stroke, though the sun has not been up an
hour. And that village dandy — how slovenly he
looks ! He is a dirty fellow, and white gloves
would look very badly on his hands now ; but he
is a plucky boy, and has got a blazing fire in his
eye and in his heart. His company will fight.
They laughed at first ; but that's all over, and now
they are ready to take their captain in their arms.
They trust him perfectly. He is in the right place
at last.

And so it is throughout the regiment. When

the two hours of fighting are over, the courage, the mettle, of each man is settled for ever; and such a climbing-up of new idols, and pulling-down of old ones, never was seen. Captains and colonels are proved not to be fit for privates; and corporals and privates have shown themselves plucky, calm, splendid soldiers. The regiment all know who is big, and who little, after that; and their estimate is not quite like that of the villagers, as they stood in line on the green in front of their homes. They know why the colonel had the colic; and that man can never control them again. Tagg is their master; and, when he nods, they obey. Capt. Blunt don't tell any more panther stories; or if, by an unlucky chance, he begins one, some innuendo puts a sudden stop to his nonsense. That two-hours' fight was like a sieve into which a shovelful of gravel had been thrown. The sieve was most terribly shaken; and, do what it would, the sand fell through, and only the pebbles remained.

It is very curious to note the diseases with which certain soldiers are afflicted when the news of an impending battle comes. While some who are in the hospital insist upon joining their regiments, others, seemingly healthy and robust, insist upon occupying the bedsteads emptied. I think there must be something deleterious in the air: for these most alarming symptoms appear; and the patient who yesterday was bullying the men of his squad has put on the most lugubrious face, and looks as though the smallest youth in the company might knock him over with impunity. He has a terrible pain in his right arm, and has dropped his musket three times while on drill; and then, again, he has a very queer feeling in his legs, and sometimes his knees will shake so that he can hardly stand up. Poor fellow! If you judge of his sickness by the length of his face and his piteous tones, you would order the company-carpenter to make a pine box at once. If the surgeon has just been enlisted, and is a little verdant, he will probably dose the boy for the next three days, and congratulate himself at the end of that time, when the battle is over, on his skill in reaching and removing disease. If he has been a surgeon before, he will either report the man as a shirk, and see that he is put in the front rank on the morrow; or else, in the kindness of his heart, will recommend a few days of perfect quiet in the hospital, his rations to be corn-meal gruel three times a day, and a blue pill every night. But what are three blue pills to an ounce of lead? To be sure, in the aggregate, blue pills have killed more than the lead: but these particular three will do no harm; for the cunning dog, who knows his own disease, the moment the nurse's back is turned, quietly disposes of the deadly ball by throwing it out of the window.

There is another class of men who go to the war, though not to fight, who ought to be noticed. When the column is formed, they are always in their places; but, when the grape comes, they are to be found in the rear with a sprained ankle, or terribly overcome by fatigue, or sitting behind a thick stump, fixing some part of the gun, which got out of order when the enemy fired the first shot, and which will not get into order again until the retreat is sounded, when its bearer will lead the advance; or, again, until the shout of victory rends the air, when he will be found among his comrades, perspiring freely, and telling of the way in which he dropped one big rebel, who would certainly have killed him if he had not — " Retreated behind a stump," says a little noiseless fairy — drawn a bead on him just as he did. There are always fifteen or twenty such fellows in a regiment, whose rhetoric, when they are at home, is of the most marvellous order; who make themselves the means of many a wretch's death; but who take precious care not to get near enough to the enemy, to do any damage, or to be damaged. They are disciples of Butler, believing that he was a logician and a philanthropist when he wrote, —

> " Those that fly may fight again;
> Which he can never do that's slain:
> Hence timely running's no mean part
> Of conduct in the martial art."

If a man who talks of the war tells you large stories, you may put it down as a mathematical certainty, that he kept out of range of the enemy's guns. There is something so terrible in a battle, the shock to the nervous system is so great, that he who has been in the thick fight seldom prates of it, never jests at it.

"He jests at scars who never felt a wound."

There is another large class of persons who are thrown to the surface by the war: I mean the vampires. These make a numerous family, and are of all possible sizes; some sucking only a few drops of blood, and others filling themselves to repletion. They are an anomalous race, and have full swing for their propensities, only when society is in confusion. They are to be dreaded, and to be hated; for they have souls so small, that the angel's microscope will hardly discover them; and so mean and corrupt, that resurrection will be simply an act of mercy. I have had occasion to watch this thrifty family, — the direct descendants of the unrepentant thief, — and am surprised at the vast number engaged, in and out of the army, in cheating. The actual first cost of subsisting our army, and of the war, is only about one-fifth of the amount stated as the national debt. The remaining four-fifths, on which rich and poor have to pay taxes, is found in the splendid equipages which fill Central Park, and in the grand houses of those who were glad enough, two years ago, to make both ends meet in a quiet house in a side-street. The stricken country begged for help, and appealed to the manhood of those whom she had blessed. Then, out of every thousand who with true chivalry emptied their purses into the treasury, and offered their lives, if they were needed, there were ten so mean and dastardly, that, while they were counting their gold, they slipped, at every opportunity, a handful into their own pockets. I long for one wholesome hour of absolute despotism. I pray for a man who shall decree, that it is an unpardonable crime to make a dollar out of a Government contract; and who will catch the first wrong-doer, and hang him high as Haman. If we were Russians, and were conscious of an antagonism between ourselves and the working head, who was prosecuting a war for his own benefit or glory, there might be some excuse for speculation: but in a country where the Government is all the people can ask, — is, indeed, just what the people themselves have made it; whose inhabitants are fighting for a continuance of those blessings which have been invaded by an enemy ruthless and anti-democratic, — it is an infinite crime for A—— to make a million dollars, and compel you and me to contribute our share towards its

payment.   He gives nothing, but sucks from the
treasury a million dollars. You give your son, and
I myself, to the war.   We both make terrible
sacrifices, and run great risks; and yet, when the
war is over, and your son is dead, and my health
gone, this Mr. A—— quietly tells us, that, of the
aggregate of the national debt, he has in his own
plethoric purse a huge amount, and that you and
I must help support his blood-horses, and pay for
his rich carpets and furniture.   These are the terrible inequalities of war.   It is a constant struggle,
not merely between the two contending armies, but
also between those who are patriots, and who pray
for vigor and decision on the part of all officers, and
these fiends who would prolong the contest, caring
neither for life nor liberty, if only they can enrich
themselves.

Nine months ago, I was young, and turned a deaf
ear to these croakings of corruption; but now I am
older, and, were ours a common war, I should be
so filled with disgust, that I should stoutly assert
the total depravity of man.   We are completely
honeycombed by money-makers.   There is no military office whose salary represents the income of
the incumbent.   By just nicking the conscience,
turning the head to one side, saying, "Poh, nonsense!" when a sensible man comes to complain of
a great outrage, the perquisites roll up in size to a

fearful bulk; and at every door, from the highest office to the lowest, there stands a villain, who is willing to pay for the favor granted any amount from five to five thousand dollars, according to the rank of the officer and the nature of the favor.

But, when I grow sick at heart as these things come to my knowledge one by one, I turn with mingled wonder and pride to the great, the glorious American people. They have never once refused Government any thing. They have never asked the President to be economical. They have heaped about him their gold, assuring him that they have plenty more when that is all spent. They have always had an infinite trust in Providence; believing, never doubting, that victory will crown our efforts at last. They have, without a murmur, borne eighteen months of successive defeats; and, with heroic patience, waited for the dawn of better times. They have given their most talented sons to stand side by side in the ranks with those of poorer birth, knowing that, in the hour of danger, we are all equal; and though, through the mismanagement and copperheadism of some of our generals, many thousand homes have been filled with weeping, no one has asked for peace, unless it be a peace based upon the unconditional surrender of every rebel flag. America, to-day, presents a magnificent sight. All her people read and think:

they are aware of the importance of the contest, and they are ready and willing to make every sacrifice. They deserve the victory; and in good time it will surely come.

I have been so much interested in the proceedings of this family of vampires, that I have spent a great deal of time in watching their skilful plans, and admiring the genius they so brilliantly display. Their strategy is perfect; their patriotism is so heavily plated, that most men are deceived thereby; and their success is so complete, that the pockets with which they commenced operations are now so well lined, that the proprietor can buy the best pew in the up-town church, and drive his dog-cart, with a servant in livery to attend his slightest wish; while a host of friends on the street smile as he passes, though they laugh when he has gone by.

The first of the family is Burly Vampire, Esq., who lives in a splendid chateau, just out of the city. In the first year of the war, he offered to sell his fine estate, and put the whole bushel of gold into the public treasury. We all looked on in wonder. Vampire must have greatly changed to do such a noble thing. His gray hairs have made him patriotic. Government smiled upon the gift and the donor; and the next year, when an expedition was to be fitted out, and a hundred vessels were needed for transportation, Vampire, Esq., said at once, that they could be furnished, and without delay. It was a huge transaction; and cost such a vast sum of money, that an extra bill of a hundred thousand dollars would not have caused any particular alarm.

Now, as Vampire sold his estate, and gave the proceeds to Government, thus showing disinterested patriotism, it was to be supposed that he would aid the Administration in this work, charging only a reasonable sum for his services. The logic is good. When you think of it, it seems very reasonable.

But look sharply, and I will show you a trick. It is no easy work to find a hundred good vessels; yet, on the fixed day, they were all floating in the harbor, ready to receive our boys. How is it, though, that so many of them were old worn-out hulks? They did not look as though they would float for twenty-four hours, without constant work at the pumps. Did our boys not deserve good accommodations on their voyage to the field of peril and death? or were there no stanch craft to be hired? It seemed as though all the ragged ends of the marine had been gathered together. Still, twenty-five thousand men embarked, and put out to sea, hopeful and happy. The land, however, was hardly lost sight of before a dozen of these craft leaked like sieves. The water oozed through the rotten plank; and, every

time a wave struck them, they trembled and shook
like a palsied old man when jostled by a full-blooded
youth.

The soldiers were disheartened at once. The
moral depression of such an incident is incalcula-
ble. Soldiers are not brutes: they are men. If
they are men, they have a right to expect that Government will pay some regard to their safety. The
demoralization commenced then and there, which
lasted all through the campaign. One of the vessels put into port before she was thirty-six hours
out; and, when that vessel anchored, she never
summoned strength enough to put to sea again.
Our boys were sea-sick, huddled together like pigs,
and at last germinated an epidemic. They were
detained thirty days before they could get proper
transportation. Other craft in the fleet put in at
Fortress Monroe, and the troops were detained six
weeks doing nothing. Still others made for Port
Royal; and so on, all along the coast.

The quiet man, while sipping his coffee of a morning, asks how Government, which pays the highest
price for every thing, could be gulled so fearfully.
I answer, Easily enough; and, if you will just step
behind the curtain, I will show you the secret. Mr.
Vampire agreed to furnish, for purposes of transportation, a hundred vessels. Rich as he was, he
owned but a dozen; and so was compelled to look

about, and find others. Now, it so happened that certain gentlemen, who were in possession of vessels which had fairly run their race, grown old and leaky in the service, being desirous of turning an honest penny, had their rotten craft overhauled, the very worst timbers (those which yield to the pressure of your finger, like a sponge) removed, and others substituted. Then they furnished them with a new coat of paint and new rigging, until, to the eye, they looked quite young again. And so they were in fresh water, or while riding at anchor; but when out at sea, bending to a strong north-easter, their old joints cracked and groaned, and the chances were that the six hundred soldiers on board would never see land again. Well, these amiable proprietors of defunct craft varnished into seeming life made an attack on the authorities at Washington, offering to loan their vessels for the very moderate sum of three hundred dollars per day. With an acuteness which is not noticed in every department, the official besieged sent a committee to examine the vessels. Before he went on board, a large-sized and exceedingly tempting greenback was offered, as a token of friendly regard, to the inspector. But he, being a *rara avis* (if Diogenes had met him, he would have blown his light out at once, and embraced him), had the audacity to refuse the bribe, and, going on board, did his duty. The vessels were not accepted. They were regarded as unseaworthy; and the proprietors had varnished their craft in vain.

When it was known, however, that Vampire, Esq., had a contract to furnish a hundred vessels, they made a second attempt. They besieged his counting-room, where he sat in state; they told him that their craft were just seven years old next spring: but he knew every vessel on the coast; and knew their owners, and what they had been doing, and that they had met with a rebuff at Washington. It did not take the two parties long to come down from rhetoric to plain matters of fact. Government would pay him for their craft three hundred dollars per day: but they could not loan the vessels directly to Government; and, unless he took them, they would prove a dead loss. So, after a great deal of sparring, it was finally agreed that he should hire their vessels at a hundred and fifty dollars each per day. He thus quietly pocketed a large fortune every month, and could throw another country-house into the public treasury.

The result was, that our boys were crowded on these sponges, which just floated, and compelled to remain in durance vile twenty-seven days in making a Gulf passage, instead of ten; which would be the case if Government would be sharp and economical enough to hire a stanch steamer at a thousand dollars per day.

That is one way in which Goverment is cheated. Millions are rolled up in the course of a few years by such contracts as this; and Government, sometimes compelled to put itself temporarily into the power of certain large business-men, is thus foully betrayed; and the poor of the whole country must pay a cent more for a loaf of bread, that the rich man may drive four horses instead of two.

If I were a member of the Ottoman Empire, and the ruler was so haughty that he disdained to look at me, — nay, if for his pleasure he put his foot on my neck, and scorned me, — I think I could laugh when he got into trouble; and, if he were so humbled that he came to me for help, I should certainly make him pay heavily, and get out of his misery as large a heap of gold as I could, and then think I had done no more than right. But when that Government which has blessed me ever since I crawled out of my cradle, which has shaped my youth, and moulded my manhood, offering me every blessing she was able to bestow, is attacked by assassins, and falls at my feet, asking me to help her in her strait, I am bound to do it by gratitude, chivalry, and honor; and if, when I have done what I could, I look into my coffers, and find an extra penny, I am a base recreant, an unfilial son, and little better than a traitor.

18

There is another class of men who are hard at work on the national debt: I mean the quarter-masters of the army. I often wondered why there was such an ambition to fill this post. It seemed to me particularly arduous and harassing, with not a large pay; and yet it seemed to be an office coveted by every one. The regiment, the post, the division, the department, each has an officer of this grade; and, curiously enough, they all come home richer than they went. The regimental quarter-master has a rather narrow circle in which to act, and so operates on a small scale. Still, if he is energetic and unscrupulous, he can do very well for himself, and make the thousand men of the regiment pay for it. Government allows so much meat, flour, &c., to each man per day. Now, the allowance is exceedingly liberal; and no man can eat a full ration. This food is, of course, received in bulk, and dealt out as demanded by the various companies. At the end of every month, several barrels of pork and salt meat, and a good proportion of all other articles of food, are unconsumed. This is greatly increased by the number of men on the sick-list, for whom full rations are drawn, though they consume nothing at all. This large quantity of material should be disposed of, and added to the regimental fund, to be expended in little delicacies for the hospital, and in a library for the convalescent. Government, you see, has a kindly care for its boys. It does not want them to suffer, and does all it can to supply every needed article of diet. But, unless the officers of the regiment are well posted on these matters (and volunteer officers seldom are), the patriotic individual who left his home and his business, that he might do the hardest work of the· regiment for a hundred and eighteen dollars a month, has been metamorphosed into a sucker, fastened on the body of the people, and filling itself with their blood. And this branch of the Vampire Family is very large. Almost every regiment has a representative; and though, when starting from home, they make to themselves fair promises to be honorable, yet, in the confusion of camp-life, the temptations come thick and fast, and, little by little, the officer's honesty melts. I know one who quietly turned all available material into greenbacks, for his own private use; while in the hospital were a score of men languishing for the want of little delicacies, and such nourishing food as his greenbacks would easily buy. There was no fund to buy such things with. In most of our regiments, this matter is most foully neglected; and the regimental sick, all over the country, will bear me out in saying, that they have been most shamefully neglected in this regard. The poor fellows who fell out of the line, and took to their beds, have many and many a time been compelled to chew a junk of hard salt meat, and to drink the black coffee without milk, when, if the colonel had been sharp, and had brought his quartermaster up with a round turn, these same boys might have had a nice piece of beefsteak and a cup of luscious tea. The worth, moral as well as physical, of a cup of fragrant tea and a steak to a worn-out soldier, you at home can never estimate. Quick as the poor fellow sniffs it, he lifts himself up, though he may not have been strong enough to do so for twenty-four hours, and pours out his thanks. There is just this difference in the two diets: Give him the salt meat and the old tin cup of coffee, and he turns over in disgust, and feels sicker than ever, — he needs something to break the weary monotony of food: offer him the tea and toast, or steak, and he eats, relishes, brightens up, and is better physically for the rest of the day. This is the reason: In nine cases out of ten, a part of the patient's disease is home-sickness: he at once feels the dreadful loss of that care which would watch over him were he at home. This loneliness depresses him, and in-creases the vigor of the disease. Now, do any thing, no matter what, to keep his spirits up, — change his food, give him delicacies, and thus show him that he is cared for, — and you do much to help the surgeon. Patients always get well sooner in hospitals where women nurse the sick. They are more like home. Now, then, what shall we say of that man who refuses to do his honorable duty, and pockets the money which belongs to these sick boys? He is an assassin, and has blood on his hands; he is a traitor and a knave, and does not deserve to be recognized by honest men: his money is all Judas-coin, and will, sooner or later, bring him to grief.

The quartermasters of every grade are thus pressed by temptation; and, when you look so high up as to see the official through whose hands the entire subsistence for a force of fifty thousand men passes, you see also various large sluice-ways, leading directly from the public treasury to that individual's private coffers. He occupies a position which is worth to him from fifty to a hundred thousand dollars a year. The vast quantity, the Ossa on Pelion, of breadstuffs, meats, &c., which are to subsist the army, should be transported at the lowest possible rates. It is this official's business to find that lowest rate, and thus to save Uncle Sam from the hands of the Philistines. But, alas! too often the official is himself a Philistine, who can trace his pedigree directly to the fallen angels of pre-Adamite times. He learns the highest rates of transportation (i.e., the rates asked

by merchants who have stanch, sea-worthy craft);
and that is the price affixed to the bill he sends to
Washington. He then finds out what he can get
transportation for from a set of pettifoggers, who
have craft like bowls, — sure to be three times the
usual number of days on the passage. The pecuniary difference between the bill in Washington,
and that in somebody's breast-pocket, is, on this
huge pile of material, something suggestive of a
small fortune. But does the shrewd official, who
has saved his country forty thousand dollars, hurry
to headquarters, and give it in for the public good?
Does he boast that he has reduced the national
debt just that amount? Or does he found an or-
phan asylum with it, a home for deceased soldiers'
children? I have never heard of such a thing. It
is possible that it may have been done; but I enter-
tain some very grave doubts. One reason why
I doubt it is this, — that, ten miles in the country,
a handsome residence has suddenly changed hands;
that the granite store, at the corner of one and
another street, has recently been sold; and I am
convinced that a quartermaster's position is a very
lucrative one.

Here is another way in which something is
added to my tax and yours. The horses of several cavalry regiments, and of all the officers of a
corps d'armée, are in want of hay. Somebody is

empowered to buy it. Great confidence is placed in the officer thus selected, and he occupies a very responsible position. He receives the money for good, sweet hay, such as our army horses ought to have. And yet, strange to say, when the hay reaches its destination, and my hostler opens my bundle, it is found to be old, with all the life dried out of it; and so musty and dusty, that, when the poor horse dives his nose into it, he makes a continuous sneeze, which runs through the entire length of his body. It is hardly fit for bedding. The poor horses refuse it, are fed on oats, get heated, and at last debilitated; and the next day, in an engagement, are all jaded, when they should be fresh; and instead of spiritedly feeling the spur, and pushing into the midst of the foe, they are sullen and unmanageable, and the battle is lost. Many and many a charge has been decided by the condition of the horses. Sometimes the rider has nothing to do but think of his sword; for the fresh animal enters into the spirit of the scene, and, knowing the bugle-calls, obeys instinctively. Again: the rider's whole time is taken up with his beast: both lose their temper, and nothing but a retreat is accomplished. Who is responsible for all this? — these lives lost, this disgrace to our arms, and perhaps the loss of a standard? Trace it back far enough, and you will find it in that

man who pretends to patriotism, but who bought
musty hay, instead of good, fresh, nourishing hay,
and made six dollars a ton by the operation; and
who would be sorry if he thought the war would
end in the next six months. We ought to have a
bloody code; and any man with shoulder-straps on,
who is caught robbing the country in this way,
should be shot in the presence of the whole army.
But nothing, as yet, has been done. We are too
kind, too lenient, too patient. We ought to be able
to check such villany: for these under-currents
are not streamlets, but deep rivers; and they are
making this debt of ours an ocean, instead of a
pond.

In speaking of our cavalry, I have noted another
fact, which has excited my indignation. When
this important arm of the service was being organized, it was ordered that no horse above a given
age (eight years) should be accepted; and an inspector, or many inspectors, men who were thoroughly versed in such matters, were well paid to
see to it that only sound, tough, and young horses
were paid for by the Government. Notwithstand-
ing this, we have thousands of horses on our hands,
eating our fodder, who are either spavined, blind,
or antediluvian. We say we pay a hundred and
twenty-five dollars apiece for all our horses: but, if
the truth were known, it would be seen that there

is hardly a horse in the service, which is sound and tough, that did not cost double that sum; because he is the only good one of two, each of which cost a hundred and twenty-five dollars.

But how is this? It is a trick of one of the vampires. It is done so easily and so skilfully, that you may look on while it is being performed, and not detect the trick. The jockey inspector is a very Herman; and you must watch him closely, or you will not discover the secret. He stands here before us, while yonder are a drove of two thousand horses. They are the scourings of the West. Some are good, some bad, some very indifferent. One would think that the order was plain enough, and that no shrewd trader would bring a blind or otherwise disabled horse to such a market. Still, here they are; and they are marched in one by one to the inspector. A good, plain, honest-looking man trots up six handsome, young, tough fellows, who look as though they could stand a long march without being fagged. The old trader is a farmer, has a hundred or two acres in Illinois, and has raised these horses himself. He knows them to be finely put together, and expects Uncle Sam will be glad to get them. He leads them up, and the inspector looks them over one by one; while the old farmer's eyes twinkle with pride, and in his heart he is inwardly praying that six brave boys

19

may get astride of them. In a few minutes, he is vastly surprised to find that they are appraised at only a hundred dollars each; for he knows them to be fully worth the twenty-five more, which is the maximum price. He, however, pockets his chagrin, and, together with you and myself, determines to see what will be the valuation of some other animals of the drove. Next comes a lank beast, which has plainly been a cart-horse for some years, and whose joints are not exactly like a pony's. At a glance, we see that he is at least twelve years old, and only wait to hear the inspector refuse him. That official looks at his teeth, feels of his legs, and then, to our chagrin and surprise, accepts him at a hundred dollars. The old farmer's eyes roll round wonderingly as he looks from this hack to his sleek ponies, and goes off evidently bewildered. It is to be hoped that the good man does not see through the trick to this day. You and I will watch a while longer, and perhaps we may get a little light.

Another drove of a dozen horses are soon brought up; and this time the owner seems to have a few private words with the inspector. What they are talking about, I cannot say. Their tones are not loud; and the gestures consist of the winking of the eye, and a seemingly friendly grasp of the hand.

'Tis very proper thus to meet as brethren : but, a minute after, I notice (for I have very quick eyes) that the inspector puts the hand which returned the jockey's friendly grasp into his pocket, — his waistcoat-pocket; and, if I am not greatly mistaken, I saw a round yellow piece of metal, that would answer well for a twenty-dollar gold-piece. Of course, I was mistaken; but I will see what becomes of the horses. The first is an unbroken, wild colt ; certainly not fit for the cavalry service until he has been tamed by curb and rein. Still he is passed at once, and the highest price paid. The four next ones are evidently hack-horses. Their ribs can all be counted ; their eyes are dull, and one, at least, is certainly blind. These, of course, will be rejected. But no ; not one of the dozen is rejected : and I am now sure of two things, — first, that I did see gold ; and, second, that the poor fellow who rides any one of these horses, will, in less than a month, wish himself at home, inwardly swearing, either that the horse is unfit for the service, or that he is unfit for a rider.

The man who owns the next drove is an honest-looking fellow, but seems to have no particular friendliness towards the inspector ; and, as a consequence, three of his horses are rejected. Now, I notice, and so do you, that all horses, good, bad, and indifferent, whose owners have such a kindly feeling for the inspector that they shake hands with him, are passed without any trouble; while those owners who neglect this ceremony take home half their animals.

It is a significant fact. Cross the villain's palm with gold, and he will make the Government pay a hundred dollars for a beast which will have to be stabled within three days for disability, and which will cost the country more for fodder before he dies than the original price paid for him. Placed in a responsible position, not only by the Administration, but by the North, by Humanity, by Liberty, to use his best knowledge, and choose only those beasts which can endure the hardships of a campaign, and bear our boys through the rugged fortunes of war to victory, the jockey sells himself to the Devil, and his country to defeat, for the few paltry hundreds or thousands with which he buys a farm, or lifts a mortgage on his old place.

He is a type of a large class of men who are thrown to the surface by the war, and who are made criminals by the times. This jockey, in his own village, was a respectable man. He would cheat you out of fifty dollars, if he could, in a horse trade; but that is nothing. Now, all the inner depths and possibilities of evil in his nature have, by the great convulsion, been brought to the surface, and he has proved himself a traitor and a villain. " Power," says the Greek Chilo, — " power discovers the man." Many a man needs but the opportunity, the temptation, to become a fiend. Such men the war has belched up from the depths of society; and they would disgust us with ourselves, and with humanity, were it not that bright examples of highest heroism in the field, and of noble self-sacrifice at home, loom up in the dusty horizon, as stars sometimes break through the clouds at night, and light our pathway with their hallowed rays.

Gold is the "Open sesame" to most men's hearts. Unless one is strongly intrenched behind the solid works of Christian truth, he runs great risks every hour. Once in a while, we see a splendid instance of heroism; and, close upon its heels, an instance of unfaithfulness, which makes us sad for our country.

While a company was placed on guard at an outpost beyond Carrollton, attempts were constantly made to smuggle goods to the enemy through a bayou that ran by their headquarters. One night, the soldier on duty was startled, as he walked his quiet beat, by the rustling of some bushes near him. He stopped, listened, heard nothing; and, concluding that he had been mistaken, resumed his walk. Soon he heard the same sound, and, in addition, the crackling of a twig. "Who goes there?"

he cried; and, receiving no answer, called the corporal of the guard, who at once sent out his men. They soon returned, bringing with them a youth dressed in citizen's clothes. He was taken before the lieutenant in command; when it was discovered that he was an officer in the Confederate army, who had wealthy parents living in New Orleans, whom he had not seen for more than a year. Feeling extremely homesick, he determined to attempt to pass our lines. He borrowed or bought a suit of citizen's clothes; and, after secreting himself in the woods a few days, found an opportunity to pass our pickets. He had been with his parents thirty days, and was now attempting to repass the pickets on his return. Poor fellow! He felt badly enough at being caught; for, according to the rules of war, he would be regarded as a spy, and shot. Fearing this penalty, he begged hard that his father might be sent for. The lieutenant, at length, moved by his entreaties, sent an orderly with a message to the city. The father arrived in due time; and, in an instant, saw the peril into which his son had fallen. He tried all the arguments a fond father could summon to persuade the lieutenant to allow his son to go free. The faithful officer was deaf to all his entreaties: he seemed like stone, and the hot words and eloquent entreaties seemed like spray dashing against the granite cliff. At last, in perfect desperation, the father took out his note-book, wrote a check for ten thousand dollars, and presented it to the officer with —

" Take this, sir, and the bank will give you the money to-morrow. You have but to turn your head, to leave the room for three minutes, and my boy can escape in the darkness."

Then, with Roman virtue, his poverty unmoved by the tempting bribe, — his widowed mother and lovely sisters in their humble New-England home seeming, but only seeming, to plead for the life-long comfort which could be bought by a moment's inadvertence, — he turned sternly to the tempter with —

" No, sir: I do my duty at all hazards."

I wish that this was the end of the incident. " But the trail of the serpent is over them all." There seems to be no bright picture of daring, of self-sacrifice, but it has on its back the stern tracings of something mean and base. This lieutenant was taken to the proper authorities in the city, and delivered up. Imagine the surprise of the whole picket-force, when, three days afterwards, he presented himself before his captors, and showed a pass, properly signed, giving him permission to go at his pleasure beyond the Federal lines ! One thing is sure: the ten thousand dollars did not find the same unmoved virtue in the city, which marked the commander of the picket-guard. The persevering father had found a man who had left his home, not for country, but for self; who did not care if the rebel officer did lead his company against our flag; and who was ready to fill his pocket-book with the price of many a soldier's life.

So the pictures stand side by side, — the good and heroic, the bad and cowardly. We find engaged in the same work the apostle of Liberty, the young enthusiast, and the Judas, who clutches the money-bag, and cares nothing for the cause of the Nazarene. These contrasts all exist in the community in time of peace ; but they are down below the surface, and only the initiated know of them. In time of war, they are thrown suddenly, and in glaring colors, upon the canvas of our history, like the magnified pictures from a camera.

Another class of men, who have attracted my attention, is the Provost-marshals. They form a family of bipeds, distinct from all other human beings. They occupy a very important position, — having almost supreme control over many miles of territory ; and are able, if so inclined, to do much harm. Capt. Vander, a restless, poor, and ambitious young man, who came to the war to make a dollar, who will never be the means of causing any one's death, and who will be very careful to keep out of danger himself, at last succeeded in wriggling his way out of his regiment, and securing for himself the provost-marshalship of an up-river parish. When I said he was poor, I meant that he had been engaged in a small retail business before the war; that his expenses exceeded his income; and that he left home in debt. He has enjoyed his new-found office just six months; and yet, on a captain's pay, he sports a thousand dollars' worth of jewelry on his person, drives a handsome span of horses, and has lent several responsible individuals five hundred dollars each. When I see his rich apparel, I become greatly interested, and begin to think, that, in a provost-marshalship, there is more machinery than I knew of. So, with candle in hand, I determine to enter the labyrinth, and find out its intricacies. A few days suffice, and I see it all. The money is easily made, if only one's conscience has been well tanned. A man must put aside all remembrance that his comrades are dying, that his regiment is in the thick of the fight, and that America expects every man to do his duty, and all such flowers of rhetoric. Like cobwebs, they must be swept away, as things disagreeable to look upon. Patriotism is a luxury not to be indulged. He must wear a pair of spectacles, which have half-dollars instead of glasses, and then all will be well.

Capt. Vander finds no difficulty in doing this. A man came to him, and a conversation something like this ensued: —

"What do you want, sir?"

"A pass to fish on the lake, sir."

"You can't have it. I'm busy: be off!"

Soon, on his desk, rings a twenty-dollar gold-piece. This means business. It is not enough, however; and the captain shakes his head. So the fisherman puts another and another, each more reluctantly than the last, until there are five shining pieces on the desk. The fellow stops short as he drops the fifth, with a dogged air, as much as to say, "No more." Vander looks through his half-dollars, and, without saying a word, writes a pass for the applicant to fish anywhere on the lake.

It is a little remarkable, but the fisherman passes our lines late in the afternoon, instead of early in the morning; and, now that I am clairvoyant, I see, in the lining of his lugger, a large quantity of silks, cottons, fine goods of various kinds, which I doubt not will be very acceptable to the rebels; while, to my surprise, I find not a single hook or line anywhere in the boat. It is a very curious circumstance.

Again: the pickets bring in a man who is suspected of smuggling. He has sold his load, and is trying to get home again; but the sharp picket

scents him out. All his effects are laid before
Vander. Here is a large roll of Confederate notes;
and here, tightly sewed up, are a thousand dollars in gold. The poor smuggler stands trembling
before his inquisitor, and expects every moment
to be taken out and shot. He is an ignorant fellow, a Creole; and, if he gets off with a whole skin,
will think himself very fortunate. Vander returns
him the worthless notes, giving him permission
to keep his boat; but puts into his own pocket the
pile of gold, sternly rebuking the trader, and, in
the heat of pretended passion, swearing to hang
him if he is ever seen in the parish again.

Here is his last act; and, thank justice, the last
one before being court-martialed. Though a young
man, he is without any of the enthusiasm or chivalry which belongs to youth; and is, or professes
to be, so conservative, that he hates the negro, and
believes in the divine character of slavery. Thus
he is the ready tool of the planter, and by far the
most popular man on the coast. He enters deeply
into the feelings of the slave-owner, and secretly
connives at the corporal punishment of the black
man, which has been abolished by law. So month
after month passes, each new one finding him more
entangled with the planters; until at last, feeling
secure in his position, and a little independent
because he has coined so much money out of his

position, he fires the mine under him, and comes down with a crash. A negro had been maltreated by his owner, and ran away from the plantation, determining to enlist as a soldier. He made for the Provost's, and stated his grievance and wish. Instead of receiving him as he should, Vander took him by the collar, kicked him out of his office, and bade him go back to his master. This was really a chivalrous act. He could not have done better had he been a real planter, instead of a planter's lackey.

The negro, persistent in his determination to enter the army, staid in the woods for eight days, living as best he could, and, every night, trying to pass the pickets and get to the city. At the end of that time, he was discovered, caught, and brought before Vander, who at once recognized him, and whose master — Vander's and the slave's — had more than once urged that search be made for the runaway. The only crime of the negro was, that he would not allow the overseer to hold the whip over his back. He had the spirit of a freeman; had felt too long the chains of slavery; and, now that the Yankees had come to protect him, insisted upon being treated like a man. On this condition, he was willing to work on the plantation; otherwise, he claimed the right to enlist in the army. He was judged, not by an exasperated Southerner, who chafed at the Yankee victories over the rebel flag, but by a *thing*, an inquisitorial biped, whose soul was all shrivelled up and withered by the wines and flattery of the chivalry. He passed the following sentence, which was carried into execution: "First, that the negro receive twenty-four lashes on his bare back; second, that he be placed in the stocks for eighteen hours; third, that he receive twenty-five lashes more; and, fourth, *that his shirt be stripped off, and his hands tied to a tree, and that he remain in that condition for three hours after nightfall, that the mosquitos, which fly in swarms, may bite him.*" I can hardly believe what I am writing; but I received these facts from Gen. Bowen, who had preferred charges against Vander, and removed him. Legree is no longer the exclusive property of the South. A young man can be so managed, after a few months' careful manipulation by the planters, that he can be made to do an act which renders his name a byword and a reproach everywhere. In the eagerness to make money, one will forget his God, his country, and even himself. But such gold has no value. Behind every bag is a spectre, the avenging shade of a faithful soldier, who was dying for the flag while this man was disgracing it; and he spends not a single dime, but he is startled by the ghostly warning, — " Remember how that gold was bought! it is the price of my life, and of your own soul." I do not envy Vander his thoughts. He must feel lonely at night; and, live long as he may, he knows he is a coward, and dares not look an honest boy in the face. There is a price fixed for every thing; and the highest price we ever pay is for gold dishonestly won. I will live on in my poverty, and be happy. He may sweep by me in his splendid carriage; but I only smile on him. Gilded panels and soft cushions are not enough to give repose. These are all forgotten whenever the flag waves in the breeze, and covers all honest men with its benediction. It fills him with remorse, and he is miserable, while I rejoice. I gave to my country all I could: he took all he could from her.

There is still one other family of bipeds in this great menagerie, well worthy our attention and study. They are marked by very peculiar characteristics. They are the ones who are best typified by a figure holding a huge ball of red tape in one hand, while the other grasps a pair of shears. The West-Pointer, when he understands the spirit of routine, and, in a gentlemanly way, insists that it shall be complied with, is a most invaluable personage; for his clear head and quick eye detect at once the coming snarl in events, and his active fingers apply the remedy. But, on the other hand, when, being a man of only mediocre ability, he has never sought this spirit, and insists on the strict letter of routine, cursing you, because, carrying a message of life or death, you came to the office on the full run, when you should have walked in a dignified way, regardless of consequences, he is a public and a private bore. In the war, this family has a factitious value; and to have graduated at West Point is to be looked upon with a sort of awe. There is many a man, who, when he receives his diploma as a full-fledged A.B., cannot pass the examination, and enter the freshman-class again; and, unless West Point is unlike all other institutions of learning, it gives to the world, with every class, some men who are good mathematicians, who can tell you all about fortifications, are perfectly acquainted with all necessary branches of military learning, but who have not, and never will have, what is *nascitur non fit*, i.e. common sense.

What the Sadducees were to the Jews, these West-Point men are to our army, — the exclusives, the aristocracy; those who look down on volunteers as mere stuff, and who laugh at men who are not posted in tactics, but who yet will often lead where these men dare not follow. The knowledge how to do a thing, and the ability to do it, are not always combined; and scattered through our army are numerous young men, whose only point of superiority above ten thousand others is that they have graduated at West Point. This is enough to excuse their blunders, their insults, and their unendurable superciliousness.

I know one such. When a colonel, whose sick men had been four days without a physician, went to ask that a surgeon might be sent to them, he was turned off with, " Oh ! they are nothing but nine-months' men. Go on, driver."

This may be according to the Army Regulations ; but it is contrary to the dictates of humanity, and an insult to every nine-months' man in the department.

I know another, who is so enamoured of the way in which he always has proceeded, that he refuses to sign a soldier's discharge until the pile of discharge-papers has reached a fixed height. Now, it is often of the utmost consequence that the discharged boy be sent North at once. Twenty-four hours, forty-eight hours, may make a serious difference in the chances of his recovery. He never can get well in the South; but send him to his home in the North, and the fresh air, and loving presence and attendance of friends, bring new life, and are better than any medicine in the surgeon's chest. Yet this man has been known to retain discharge-papers in his possession so long, that many and many a time, when the papers were at last signed, the poor boy was safe from West Point, and in the ground. The reason is, that the routine, once fixed upon, must not be changed: it must yield neither to right nor wrong, to God nor the Devil.

The youthful West-Pointer, when he is in full feather, honestly believes that it was the Army Regulations, and not the Decalogue, which came from the mysterious cloud to the children of Israel. The law written therein is harder than that of Mede or Persian. The order, once issued, must not be retracted. While lying in New-York Harbor, one of these gentlemen issued an order to the pilot of the boat to start at three, P.M., precisely. The captain, knowing that the vessel could not get off before five, P.M., was ashore.

"We cannot start at that time, sir; for the tide does not serve."

"The order has been issued, and you will obey it."

The half-frightened pilot, never thinking that the captain was ashore, gave the order at three precisely, and the vessel began to move. The tide was low; but what of that? Shall a West-Point graduate retract an order simply because its execution is impossible? Nonsense! The vessel swung partly round; when all at once she ran her stern into a mud-bank, and was immovable.

Now, you may issue as many orders as you choose: you must wait quietly until the tide serves. In about half an hour, the captain went on board, and swore, as only an old sea-dog can, in a voice that might be heard all over the harbor; cursing the pilot for his want of common sense, and sending him off the vessel at once.

That is the side of West Point we do not want. Mere dead, dull routine, when there is no spirit in it, is the deadest and dullest thing in the world; and the Army Regulations, when followed out according to the letter by one who has not brains enough to understand their spirit and the exigencies which called them forth, are most insipid and meaningless. Brains and West Point are very well; but West Point without brains is too much of a burden for volunteers. The truth is, that we, having on our hands a war of such appalling magnitude, and knowing nothing of military matters, have placed undue confidence in any and all who profess to know how to lead us aright. In this way, many have worked themselves into high positions, who are conspicuous only for their blunders. We have been patient, and even enduring: but, now that we have had two years' experience, we are beginning to see into the darkness for ourselves; and soon we may hope for guides who will not sacrifice a victory to a point of etiquette, but who will sacrifice every thing for success.

To know every thing is not enough: to do something will soon be the only title to our respect.

These are some of the men thrown to the surface by the war. They have taken advantage of the general chaos to fill their own coffers, or to work themselves into prominent positions. But a small man in the midst of a large fortune is a pitiable object; and a minute man, clothed in a gaudy uniform, and strutting about in the place which should be occupied only by the great head and great heart, is certainly not to be envied. Poor fools! they will checkmate themselves before they have made many moves. And these are a few of the ways in which the national debt is rolled up. There are others, scores of them, which I know nothing about. Indeed, there must be; for the patent cost of subsisting and paying our army seems a small sum by the side of what we actually expend every month. I was greatly interested in this matter, and wondered — this was in the days of my blissful ignorance and verdancy — how our bills amounted to something like a million a day. One does not remain long in the army, however, no matter how quiet the position he occupies, without seeing exactly how this thing is achieved. It is not done by the soldiers who have been oftenest in the fight: if it were, we should be disinclined to criticise. They risk their lives every hour; their strong arms are repelling the invader, and establishing our homes on a safe foundation; are giving security to our commercial interests, and saving the national credit. If they all made a competency, a complaint would come with an ill grace from us. But it is not so. Those who do their duty best get only the thirteen dollars a month, and seldom bring home any other memento of the war than a wound in the breast, or a wooden leg. All honor to the volunteer rank and file! The noblest patriotism in the country is to be found there. They are the most disinterested men we have, and should be held in the warmest regard. The people have vindicated their right to republicanism. The thoughtful, honest, self-sacrificing people are to-day showing the world in how high estimation they hold our free schools and our free government. They have rushed with irresistible force against the monarchists of the South; and, in the shock of battle, are silencing the croaking rhetoricians of Europe, who have predicted that republicanism was in its death-struggle. So far from the truth are they, that, on the other hand, our victorious flag will yet give a new impulse to all the liberty-loving men of Europe. It will say to those beyond the great sea, " Struggle on, brave Italians and noble Poles : your cause is God's cause and man's; fight on, and you shall yet be free."

It is not necessary that I should tell you in whose pockets this immense amount of money finds a resting-place. They are men who have no other than a financial interest in the war, — the most unworthy and unpatriotic. I have given an imperfect catalogue of some of them, and am glad to reach the end of a very disagreeable subject. Heaven help them! I say; for they have had no mercy on themselves. In spite of them and their ill-gotten gains, the cause treads with firm step, and the end is approaching; and, when glorious peace — a peace won by struggle and by blood — shall crown our borders once again, these men will take their rightful place: they will form a clique with no inward sense of satisfaction, but with a feeling of utter degradation; while those who gave of their substance, and of the best fruit of their lives, will walk proudly under the benedictive red, white, and blue, and say, "It is ours, — our own; for we paid the sacrifice, and won it."

CHAPTER VI.

ON THE MARCH.

I CASUALLY heard, one day, that the army was soon to march upon Port Hudson; and at once went to the general, and asked and obtained permission to postpone my work for a while, and accompany him. It was a bright, beautiful morning when the command was given, " To horse, gentlemen ! " and the noble Farragut had passed Baton Rouge in the "Hartford," cheered by the huzzas of ten thousand hearts. He is really a hero; and there is a ring to his tones, which reminds one of a trumpet, when he says, " Iron gun-boats are all well enough ; but give me a crew of iron hearts." We very soon caught up with the advancing column; and I have never witnessed a grander sight than that presented by our forces. First a wagon-train, interminable in length, filling up the road for full two miles, — the white canvas tops contrasting with the rich green of the foliage, for the road was through a dense wood; the drivers hallooing to their mules; the negroes making the woods ring with their songs: all made up a picture at once novel and interesting.

Next we came upon a solid column of some twenty-five thousand men. They were in the best of spirits; and as the whole body parted in the middle, and filed to either side of the road, and gave expression to their confidence in their leader by cheers which ran along the entire length of the line, every one was roused to an enthusiasm almost uncontrollable. I felt that he who led such a body of men was the most enviable being in the world; and, when the scene was rendered wilder by the crashing music from a dozen brass bands, it seemed as if every man was ready to risk his life in the dread encounter.

That night, our advance encamped within six miles of the enemy's works. I accepted the kind invitation of Col. Bullock, of the Thirtieth, to share his tent; and slept as comfortably on the dry grass and dead leaves as though I had had a bed of down. A hard ride of six or eight hours naturally inclined me to hunger and sleep. I relished a pile of crackers and cheese more than Vitellius ever did his dainty dish of birds' tongues; and was soon afterwards on my back, giving good evidence of my condition.

I slept soundly until about half-past ten; when a faint, booming sound awoke me. It occurred at regular intervals of about a minute; and, as soon as I gathered my scattered senses, I knew that the gunboats were hard at work. I lay quietly for some time, awed by the solemnity of the occasion; for it was then pitch dark, and the dull, heavy sound was freighted with success or defeat; and, on opening my eyes again, I could distinctly trace the course of the shell through the air by the light of the fuses. I watched them until about two o'clock; when I ordered my horse, and set out for head-quarters. It was so dark that I could not keep the road, and so trusted to the instincts of my noble beast. It was, withal, a lonely ride, — five miles through dense woods, the silence only broken by the gruff " Who goes there ? " of the guard, and the ominous clicking of the hammer as he cocked his gun. All the legends of the Hartz Mountains ran through my mind; for the night seemed just fitted for a carnival of the Genii.

I had just reached headquarters when the welcome news came, that a part of the fleet had succeeded in getting by the fort. Still there was something ominous in a certain glare of light, which ever and anon burst up from the tree-tops in the distance. One of our vessels must have caught fire. It could not be a common gunboat, for the flames had already lasted several hours. At last a courier came, saying that the " Mississippi" had caught fire. That noble vessel was part of the price we were to pay for the victory hoped for.

I have never witnessed a scene so magnificent as that which closed the career of this war-ship. One moment, the flames would die away, and then the black darkness of the night seemed heavier than ever; in another minute, the flames would curl up again above the tree-tops, and tinge the cloud-edges with a lurid light. At length came the catastrophe. I thought the fire had gone out; and was just turning away, when fold after fold of cloudy flame, driven with terrific force, rose higher and higher, until the entire heavens were illuminated, as though the sun itself had burst; and immediately after came a sound that shook the earth, — a crash so awful, that it seemed as though one could feel it; which thundered along the entire horizon, frightening the birds in their coverts and the horses in their stalls; and then all was still and dark. The "Mississippi" was no more. That noble vessel, which had made for herself a history, had at last fallen a victim to the chances of war. She was a splendid ship; and every American will remember with regret the hour when she was lost.

That night, fortune did not favor me. I had escorted Col. Clarke, who had been wounded, beyond our lines, on the Baton-Rouge road; and, a second time, accepted the hospitality of Col. Bullock. I was quietly and with great zest gnawing a beef-bone, wondering at the novelty of a soldier's life, when I was surprised out of my dream by the patter of rain. I was fully prepared for fine weather; but rain I had not reckoned upon. The ground was so low and marshy, that, in the course of the first half-hour, there were at least three inches of water on it. I perched myself on a bread-box, however, crossing my legs *à la Turc;* feeling that delightful indifference to all fortune, which is the charm and necessity of a soldier's life. My bone and my hunger were enough to occupy all my thoughts. My inner man, astonished at the utter neglect of the last eighteen hours, was determined that I should concentrate my attention upon one only thing. That luscious beef-bone, which, only a few hours before, had been trotting about gayly in those very woods, seemed to me the richest luxury in the world. As I held it firmly in my left hand, and ever and anon tore from it a delicious morsel, you could not have bought it of me for a whole township.

When I had satisfied my hunger, I began to recognize the fact, that the tent was pitched in four inches of water, and that it was raining most lustily. I splattered out, tied my horse under a large tree, laughed heartily at the look of perfect surprise he put on as I turned to leave him, and then hunted until I came across a stretcher which would lift me just six inches from the ground, and serve very comfortably for a bed. Fortune did indeed favor me. I was two inches above the water, and had a covering above my head, which only once in a while played the sieve, and showered me. I slept soundly, as only the tired man can. In the morning, my faithful horse waked me with his neighing; and, if he had had the power of speech, I do not doubt he would have scolded me well for leaving him all night in a pond.

I was surprised at the uniform cheerfulness of the men under these trying circumstances. They had no covering except their rubber-blankets, which they stretched out — a very poor roof — upon four upright stakes. They were, most of them, drenched to the skin. Yet around the camp-fires were heard only mirth and wildest hilarity. Once in a while, I came across some poor unfortunate, who had dropped his blanket in the mud, and down whose back the rain was trickling mercilessly; and who seemed (I judged from the forcible expletives used) to have arrived at the sage conclusion, that a soldier's life is not always gay, as generally represented, and that camp-life and camp-meeting are two very different things. But even he soon gathered his muddy vestments about him; and, crawling alongside the bright fire, got into a better humor with himself and the fortunes of war.

When we returned to Baton Rouge (for it seems
our advance upon Fort Hudson was only a feint to
compel the enemy to withdraw their water-batteries, that Farragut might the more easily run the
gauntlet), my friend Gen. Dudley was ordered to
make a reconnoissance on the west side of the river,
and to get as nearly opposite Port Hudson as was
practicable. I received permission from Gen. Banks
to act on Dudley's staff *pro tem.* We started late
in the afternoon, three steamboat-loads of us; and,
as I wanted to reserve myself for the next day's
work, I went to bed soon after sundown, and slept
soundly until the next morning. We should have
reached our landing-place in about three hours: so
I may be excused, if, when I woke, I was surprised
to find it morning, and myself on board the steamboat. I leapt out of my berth, and scrambled for
the deck to ascertain the solutions of the mystery.
On looking about me, my first feeling was one of
chagrin; but, on second thoughts, I burst out into
a hearty laugh. It seems, that, during the night, a
heavy fog came up, and the pilots lost their way.
As luck would have it, we stopped our engines just
at the mouth of a huge crevasse. The unfortunate
steamboats were drawn in by the force of the current; and, at the precise moment when I took my
observation, the " Empire Parish " was at least a
hundred yards inside the levee, while the " Morn-

ing Light" was anchored in the very centre of a plantation, and close to a huge sugar-house. After a vast deal of cursing on the part of the pilots, and a loss of some twenty-four hours, we managed to get into the river again; and, shortly afterwards, came to a landing at Winter's Plantation. The enemy's works were plainly visible. They were only about five miles off; and, with the glass, we could distinctly see the rebels hurrying to and fro.

I was very much interested that evening in watching the soldiers, and seeing the way in which they accommodated themselves to their situation. The moment the company lines were marked out, a certain number made for the fields where the cattle were grazing; while another party proceeded to demolish the fence about the house; first, to use it for a mattress on which to sleep; and, second, for fire-wood. In less than thirty minutes from the time of landing, the fence had entirely disappeared; and to look on the men at their fires, busily cooking, or washing tin plates, or lying on the grass singing and reading, while here and there was one who carried his fiddle, and most perseveringly and pleasantly cajoled the hours away, you would have thought that they had lived on the place for weeks. They managed, in the most marvellous way, to make themselves at home. One is down by the water's edge: he has taken his

shirt off (for the day is very warm), and is scrubbing
the thing in the most determined manner. Another
has brought a rocking-chair out of the house, and
sits at his ease, watching the progress of dinner.
Others have grouped together, making very respectable music. Others, again, are in the ring;
and, judging from the black eyes and bloody faces,
have got as far as the tenth round. Fifteen minutes ago, if you had listened, you would have heard
a most ominous cackling from all quarters at once :
now not a solitary cackle can be heard within a
mile. Thirty minutes since, the lowing herd were
winding very rapidly over the lea, evidently under
the impression that danger was imminent : now
four beef-hides hang gracefully from as many
stakes, drying for the New-Orleans market, and
anxious to be converted into Yankee shoes.

At first, my heart revolted at such destruction
of life : but when, by chance, my attention was
called to a savory dish which my contraband was
lustily stirring ; and when, grinning from ear to
ear, Tom said, " Lieutenant, will you pick a chicken
bone ? " — I must confess that I forgot all things
else, my revolted feelings, and my knife and fork,
and devoured, as only a hungry man can, the better
part of a chicken ; believing all the time that the
said biped had at last accomplished its intended
mission. So my contraband must have thought ;
for when I inquired, —

"Tom, by the way, how came you by that chicken?" he answered, —

"Why, master, he want doin' no good whare he wer: so I tho't that I would put him whare he would do good."

I have never since felt any repugnance about taking whatever I wanted for subsistence from the enemy.

This sleeping out of doors, lying down in the very lap of good Mother Earth, is a glorious habit. We, who had always slept in the third-story back of a brick house, with no prospect from the window but four feet square of blue sky above, and, below, a city grape-vine, trying to live in spite of the three cart-loads of loam which were deposited years ago, and have never been disturbed since, though they are now as hard as sand-stone, — I say, one who has spent the glorious nights in such a room, and who has never allowed the window to be open more than three inches, can hardly conceive of the luxury of sleeping on the broad bed of earth, which graciously sends its fragrance of hemlock and mint to lull you to repose, and of having all the air there is to be breathed. I have often felt that one of the heaviest prices we pay for civilization, and the privilege of living in the temperate zone, is the necessity of sleeping within-doors. In the East, the best room is that which has the roof of the house for its floor, and the wide heavens for a ceiling. The poor Indian, who knows neither how to read nor write, gets closer to Nature than you or I in our artificial life. He strikes out from the beach, and swims for a mile, cutting the life-giving water with his strong arms, and taking in health and vigor at every pore; and, when night comes, he makes a bed of freshly-cut hemlock, under the protecting branches of some old tree, and sleeps so sweetly and soundly, that, in the morning, he is young again.

It is well known that our soldiers are never so well as when on the march. The reason is obvious. It is because they have healthy exercise, generally good food and pure air, and have no time to indulge in the bad habits which characterize the camp. I believe that sleeping in tents is one great cause of illness; for it frequently happens that the miasma within the tent is worse than that without. In a common Sibley tent, ten or more soldiers are compelled to take up their quarters. At night, they lie like the spokes of a wheel, the feet towards the hub, which is the tent-pole. Generally very improvident, they close every aperture before retiring; and, in less than two hours, the air has all been inhaled and exhaled. In the course of the next six hours, it undergoes the same process three times. With all creation to breathe in, the soldier persists in occupying as small a space as possible, and in being strangely economical of air. Hence it is that the lazy camp-life is more injurious and more demoralizing to troops than the march or the battle-field.

On the night of which I speak, the moon shone though the green foliage, and lighted up our camp; while the fires which were built here and there, the blue-coats hurrying to and fro on important culinary business, and the groups of singers filling the woods with the rousing tones of the "Star-spangled Banner" or some other patriotic air, served to render the scene at once picturesque and romantic.

The next morning we heard that the "Mononga-hela" was going to try her new gun. I was very desirous of seeing the effect of her shell: so some half-dozen of us mounted our horses, rode up the levee about four miles, then dismounted, and crept up under the levee, until we were immediately opposite the lower batteries of the enemy. The air was so calm, that we could hear them shouting as the gunboat came steaming up. We were within range of their rifles; and, under ordinary circumstances, should have skedaddled most ingloriously. But the attention of our well-wishers on the other side of the river was too much occupied with the frowning gunboat to take heed of us. We sat quietly on the bank of the river, in a good position for observation. The " Monongahela " was at first full four miles off, and her shell flew without any great degree of accuracy. When, however, she steamed up to within two miles and a half, she did good execution. The shell came whizzing through the air, making us instinctively cringe ; and struck within a circle two hundred feet in diameter. The workmen at the fort, with becoming bravado, at first kept on with their shovels and picks. But once a shell burst just over their heads, — not twenty feet in the air ; and such a scrambling for the house never was seen. Pell-mell, one over the other, for fear a second shell should overtake them, they hurried on. When safely lodged in the house, they seemed out of danger. But, in a few minutes, another well-directed shell burst just over the ridge-pole ; and, like a covey of frightened birds, they fluttered out of the house in most admirable confusion, and made for the woods. The Yankee gun had scared them well ; for it was full two hours before a man was again seen on the works.

Early the next day, we started on our reconnoissance, — two regiments, and a section of artillery. We went thus in force, because the reports concerning the number of rebels on that side of the river were very contradictory. Capt. Youngblood, of the signal-corps, had been taken the previous evening, together with four of his men. They were very much chagrined at their capture, and evidently attempted to mislead us as much as possible. We had not gone more than half a dozen miles, however, before we learned all we wanted to know. The negroes were our informers. With joy indescribable, they rushed out of their cabins at our approach, expressing the fervor of their feelings in every conceivable way. " God bress you all ! " cried an ancient and sooty dame, holding her hands up to give us her benediction. While the whites on the plantation looked and talked as impudently as they dared, telling us all sorts of stories to confuse us, the darkies would gather round, listening, and, every once in a while, give vent to their surprise at their master's mendacity by the most ludicrous rolling-up of the eyes, and by clasping their hands, with the ejaculation, " O Lord ! what is white fokes coming to ? "

After having interrogated the planter sufficiently, we often turned to question the negroes ; and generally learned the exact truth. At least, it was always evident that they desired not to mislead. We could trust them implicitly on all common points. They knew whether there were any rebels in that parish ; and, if there were, where they were stationed. But we never could trust their estimate of distance or numbers. They do not seem to know the difference between one mile and six, and are as likely to say five hundred as fifty. This defect is quite universal.

The negro, however, was, without a single exception, the friend of our army. He would never hesitate to give the required answer, whether it pertained to the rebel force, or even the private affairs of his owners. Many and many a time have we gone up to the master with —

" Where are your horses, sir ? "

And he has answered with infinite *naïveté*, —

" My horses, sir, have all been taken by the Confederates. The last one was stolen yesterday morning."

And, when we got out to the gate, some sable boy has quietly said, " De ole master say de hosses all gone; but I know where dey is. I find 'em for you, if you come wid me."

The result has been, that, in the course of half an hour, from one to four valuable horses have been taken from their covert in the woods, and added to our force.

Every plantation is bounded on the back side by heavy woods; and here is a convenient hiding-place for all property that ought not to meet the public eye.

I was sent up to one house, at about eleven, A.M., to say to the planter that twenty of our officers would dine with him in two hours.

"Well, sir, I suppose I must cook a dinner for you," he said in very surly tones.

"Yes, sir," I replied. "*Must* is the proper word, under the circumstances."

"Well, what shall I give you? I have a lot of salt meat in the house: will that do?"

"Hardly," I answered. "We are not accustomed to that kind of food; and some of our officers are very dainty, and inclined to dyspepsia. I see you have fowls and turkeys in abundance. I think they would serve our turn very well. Be sure, if you roast them, to have them well browned, with a great deal of dressing."

I knew my man, of course; and so did the general when he sent me there. His house had been the favorite rendezvous of the guerillas for a long time, and we feared that they had fared sumptuously. Why should he not feed us as well as he did rebels? So I turned; and, when I got to the gate, I called on old auntie, and said, "Auntie, in two hours we want dinner. Don't forget that we are friends." The old woman chuckled, and rolled up her eyes as she replied, "Master, you better b'leve none of us will forget dat." I was never in my life more certain of having a good dinner.

We rode long and hard that day, swimming our horses over the bayous, and getting ourselves into a most delightfully drenched condition. At the end of the two hours, we had learned what we wanted to know, — that there were only a few guerillas on that side of the river; and that the crevasse caused by the cutting of the levee by the rebels, when they learned of our landing, was impassable. When we reached the aforementioned house, we were greeted by a dinner such as a soldier has no right to see every day. Turkeys, ducks, and chickens, roasted, boiled, and broiled, with a most charming absence of salt meat, met our delighted vision. The old auntie had put on the table the very best the house afforded. The best dishes, forks, and spoons were all paraded; and, in their eagerness to serve us, at least a dozen of the negroes insisted on waiting on the tea-table. They fairly crowded the old master and mistress out of the room; for they soon, in high dudgeon, retired to the gallery to meditate on the natural bashfulness of the Yankee character.

The people in all this region were the worst kind of secessionists: still, we never failed to give them an opportunity to repent of their political sins before applying the extreme rigor of the law. Lieut. Fuller, of Gen. Dudley's staff, was very efficient and acute in the administration of military justice. He would halt his squad of men just out of sight of a rich planter's house, then ride up to the door, and knock; and this is the kind of conversation which generally transpired. It is at once instructive and amusing.

"Is Mr. —— within?"

"He is."

"Tell him I would like to see him."

Mr. —— soon made his appearance, looking very red, and demanded the lieutenant's business in haughty tones.

"I have come, sir, to inquire," the lieutenant would say in his blandest manner, "if you would like to come under the protection of the United States laws, and take the oath of allegiance?"

Mr. —— generally turned redder than ever, and said in a very insolent way, —

"No, sir: I desire to do no such thing."

"Perhaps, sir, you would like a little time to consider the point," the lieutenant would rejoin, unwilling to take any undue advantage.

"No, sir: my mind is made up already, and unalterably."

"Very well, sir, that is all I want to know. Boys," calling to the squad, "you may take this gentleman's mules and horses, and see that his sugar"— perhaps he has a couple of hundred hogsheads — "is carted to the levee for shipment."

"But, lieutenant," would break in the astonished and now thoroughly awakened secessionist.

" There is no ' but,' sir, about it. You have openly avowed unalterable enmity to the United States; and I shall take from your plantation every thing which I can use for the Government, and every thing which I can sell for it."

The thing is handsomely done. Discomfited secesh slams his door, cursing himself for a fool, and the rest of mankind for knaves. The Yankees have got the better of him at last, and he certainly will die of mortification. What secessionism failed to do for him, chagrin will accomplish. Two things I like to see, — an official thoroughly in earnest, and an avowed enemy roughly handled.

This earnestness is a characteristic of Dudley. He enters into the spirit of the soldier's life, and attends to all its duties, *con amore.* He is a very strict disciplinarian; and no one can punish for a military offence like " Old Dud," as the boys call him. But of one thing they are all sure, — that, when there is work to be done, he is not found in the rear of his column.

He has one practice, however, which is altogether more interesting as a novelty than as a habit. He is accustomed to ride, late at night, through the entire line of his pickets; and woe be unto that poor fellow who is found off duty ! At Baton Rouge, our pickets are only three miles from those of the enemy, with a dense wood between; and it is doubly important that they should be on the alert. One night, at about half-past ten, he asked me to go the rounds with him. It was quite dark; and, *ergo*, favorable to our purpose. After having met with the usual fortune for an hour and a half, he asked me to attempt to pass a certain outpost, while he remained in the background. So I dodged about until I succeeded in attracting the attention of the guard by my proximity; when I heard, in a gruff voice, the —

"Who goes there?"

I was about to disregard this challenge; when the guard cried out again, —

"If yees don't stand still just where ye be, I'll see what effect a bullet will perjuce."

This threat was uttered in a tone of such decision, that I judged it best to be discreet. The picket marched me up until my body touched his bayonet-point, all the while berating me soundly for trying to play some game on him.

"Now, thin, tell me who ye be, any way, and what for ye're here."

I attempted to move to one side, being slightly uneasy; but he cried out, —

"Stand mighty still, now, till I call the corporal of the guard, or I'll see how far my bayonet will go into ye with one shove!"

I hope my courage will not be impugned if I confess that I stood very still indeed.

"Now, my good fellow," I began, "I am a brother soldier. I just want to go out for half an hour, and promise to be back. Come, I'll give you ten dollars to let me go."

"To the Divil with your ten dollars!" replied the honest son of Erin, growing very wroth.

"Well, then, I will give you fifty. Only let me pass; for I must go."

"Now, thin, you thief of a rebel," — he was evidently very indignant, — "if ye budge an inch till the corporal comes and sees who ye be, I'll just let drive at you!"

He cocked his gun; and I made no attempt to escape, as you can easily guess.

One more trial, however. "Now, look here, comrade: won't you let me pass on any conditions?"

"Not if you were the Saviour of the wurruld!— Corporal of the guard! Corporal of the guard!"

I was taken, sandwiched between two soldiers, and marched up to the guard-tent; when the general gave orders for my release, and praised the soldiers for their good conduct. It will be a long time before they forget the kind words of "Old Dud," and it will be a longer time before he gets me to go the grand rounds with him again. There is something decidedly unpleasant connected with

the bayonet exercise and the whiz of a bullet. I
know there is a vast deal of romance about them ;
but then there is some reality. I like the former,
but have a decided repugnance to the latter.

I hope that my earnestness in speaking kindly of
Gen. Dudley will not lead the reader to suppose
that I have an admiration for all the men who
occupy an equally high position of trust: on the
contrary, I am greatly chagrined at some of our
military Americanisms. I think, that in this war,
so far, every thing seems to run to a brigadier-
generalship. All diseases are pretty sure to end
there. To wear " the single star " on the shoulder
is alike the ambition of the civilian and the man of
war. If one has climbed a high mountain, and
recklessly exposed life and limb, he is at once
rewarded with a white star on a black velvet
ground, with the privilege of having about his
person a staff of cousins and aunts, — for there are
a great many old aunts who wear pantaloons, —
and two hundred and twenty-five dollars a month,
and perquisites to keep up the dignity of his position with. If a captain, with a squad of men,
wades through fifty miles of marsh, when there's a
good hard road not forty rods off, and comes into
camp all splashed with mud, with eyes wide open,
and ready tongue to tell of narrow escapes from
tripping over logs secretly hidden in the swamp

by the rebels, he is at once promoted to the command of a brigade, and sent into some obscure corner of the Republic, where there is no possibility of doing any good, and very little possibility of doing any harm. In Europe, it is considered a great honor to be promoted from first lieutenant to captain on account of good conduct in the field. High offices are reached only by slow degrees, and each successive step is won by a new proof of valor. But here we put on our favorites the seven-league boots of Jack the Giant-killer; and, at a single jump, they leap from a position where their mediocrity is not discovered to a higher place, from which they are sure to be seen to be what they are, — good lieutenants, but very bad brigadier-generals. I believe in rewarding valor: we ought to have medals, and, indeed, a thousand means of doing honor to those who have shown great courage; but surely it is not necessary to dub everybody a brigadier who fights well, and then wonder where we can send him so that he will be out of harm's way.

My feeling is, that this epidemic, or madness, has done much towards prolonging the war. The country is, to-day, over-stocked with generals. Our boys have many times been sacrificed by men who would have handled a regiment very effectively, but who have floundered about in their

brigade like a boy who has suddenly stepped into
too deep water. As proof of this, you will find,
that, when a speaker is introduced to an audience
as a general, the people by no means consider,
that therefore he is a fine military man. On the
contrary, we all know, that, if there is a captain to
be found who has been taken prisoner by the
rebels, — no matter about asking why; who has
endured a reasonable amount of suffering at their
hands, and has a glib tongue to tell his story in
country villages, and excite the inhabitants thereof
to the recruiting-point, — we act very foolishly
about him. What do we do with him? Use him
simply as a speaker? — a legitimate and necessary
part of our military machinery, — one of the fan-
ners of the flame of public feeling? Not at all.
We disgrace ourselves, and the sacred cause in
which we are engaged, by setting him at work to
raise five thousand men, and then making him a
brigadier-general to command them. It is too long
a jump. It bespeaks folly on our part, and it
recklessly imperils the lives of our noblest sons.
Another fatal consequence that follows is the constant flutter in which the newly-fledged and over-
sensitive monarchs keep themselves. Gen. Smith
is making a raid, and, forgetting the necessity for
an advance guard, — for the velvet on his shoulders is quite new, and he has not yet learned all the

ways of war, — has fallen into an ambuscade. He
does the only two things that are to be done, —
fights a little, and then retreats. Being hotly pur-
sued by the foe, he sends in terrible haste to Gen.
Brown, who has pitched his tent on a neighboring
hill, for re-enforcements. Does Gen. Brown at
once order his whole force into line, and march to
the relief of his compeer ? Not at all. He quietly
sends a messenger, asking Gen. Smith the date of
his commission. It happens to be Jan. 1, while
Gen. Brown's is Dec. 31; and so, instead of sending
relief, he gets into a towering passion, and curses
Gen. Smith for an unmilitary dog, who attempts to
give orders to his superior officers. This is all
very pretty; and, had we nothing else to do or
think of, we might deem such little quarrels very
good sport: but we have something else to do.
While these two fools are fighting about the difference between Jan. 1 and Dec. 31, our boys are
being shot down, our flag endangered, our cause
injured, and our Northern homes filled with the
shadows of death.

One thing is certain: too much cannot be said of
our rank and file, and not enough has yet been told
of our officers. The latter, take the army through,
are greatly inferior to the former. We have in the
ranks men of high social position, of culture, of
wealth, who have been moved by the loftiest patri-

otism to give themselves to their country; we
have also pure-minded country-boys, farmers' sons,
by the thousand, who were fired by a holy thought
when they said good-by to father and mother,
and the old house in which they were born; and
we have large numbers of officers, who were members of military companies at a time when they
were in greatest disrepute, and who got their position only because they were acquainted with the
rudiments of military tactics, and presented themselves at a time when we were glad to confide in
any one who told us that he knew something of the
art of war.

This, however, is gradually regulating itself.

Some time after this, Gen. Banks made his de-
monstration against the rebels opposite Brashear
City. They were too few in number to offer any
great opposition; and, being made up largely of
unwilling conscripts, did little else than effect a
masterly retreat.   At one or two places on the
road, they made a stand, but only for a short time.
I was down the river when the fight began, and
without any means of transportation. We — Chaplain Wheelock and I — hurried by rail to Brashear
City. That evening, the booming of cannon in the
distance made us very uneasy. There were no
means of getting over the bay until the next after-

noon; and, by that time, the army, which made splendid marches, was about fifty miles away. When once we got on the other side of the bay, however, we succeeded in gobbling two tenth-rate horses and saddles, and started. It was a long chase. The first afternoon, we rode thirty miles, and through a country swept clean of every thing by two armies; and the second day, after having ridden fifty-five miles, we came up with the rear division of our forces. Never did an army make cleaner work than ours. The best horses had all been taken by the Texans of the enemy; but, in their haste, they left every thing that was not easily portable. Our boys drove to the rear every pony and mule, every ox and cow and sheep. They did not leave, on an average, two chickens to a plantation. Wherever they encamped, the fences served as beds and firewood. A more forlorn and destitute set of people never were seen. Some cried, some cursed, some whined; and some, over-come with fear, hid themselves in the woods, leaving every thing to the tender mercies of the army. I could not help contrasting these times and our policy with the times and policy of two years ago in Virginia. This was war, with all its penalties and all its horrors: that was a system of fighting by which nobody was hurt, and nothing injured. I remember well, how one of our colonels had marched his men for twenty hours through mud and rain; and, having bivouacked at night on a large plantation, began to use the fences to warm and dry his boys, and cook their food. He was ordered by one of our brigadiers to stop; and was actually forced to detail a squad of men *to guard the fence*, while his soldiers went to bed cold and wet and hungry. That policy, thank God! is buried. In this department, so far, war has been only war. These very houses that were ransacked, had, each of them, a representative in the army that we were chasing; and now they were suffering the legitimate consequences of rebellion. It was my first peep into rebeldom. I was in a province and among a people recently conquered; and my eyes and ears were both busy, and my experiences were exceedingly interesting. Nothing rejoiced me more than the fact, everywhere patent, that the poorer classes — the non-slaveholding classes — are, almost without exception, on our side. The unity of the South (as I have shown elsewhere) is simply a bold figure of rhetoric. The poor are weary of the war: it has done and it promises to do them no good whatever. If the South conquers, their social position is as it was. They have always been the serfs of the rich planters, doing as they were bidden, and voting as they were advised, with no privileges, and no chance for social advancement.

If the North is successful, they see clearly that the old system of vassalage is broken up. The impassable barriers of society between the rich and the poor will be destroyed. The chances for competition in business, and the opportunities for education (they speak of this with a great deal of feeling), will be vastly increased. They are not exuberant in expressing their hopes for our triumph; indeed, how can they be? for they have each a son conscripted, and somewhere in the Southern army: but still it is evident that they understand the issues of the day as well as we. Another thing which struck me with some surprise was the general scarcity of food. The richest planters could give us nothing better than cornbread and the coarsest Texan beef. They had no coffee, and said that they had had none for more than a year. One wealthy lady, whose husband, a few days before, had run his best negroes and mules back into the country, confessed (and her eyes snapped as she did so) that she had enjoyed but two meals a day for more than six months, and those of the humblest kind. There is but little doubt that the breadstuffs of the Confederacy are very low. England and France — those immaculate champions of Liberty — have done all they could to avert the inevitable starvation by filling Texas full of edibles; but, after all, it is quite evident that all interior towns have suffered immensely for every thing except corn-meal and coarse meat.

There was very little excitement to be found in the rear of the column: so, the next morning, having changed our jaded horses for two better beasts with a kind-hearted rebel (who, however, did not seem to relish the trade so much as we), we started for the advance. We were most of the time with Capt. Williamson's company of cavalry skirmishers. This, certainly, is the most exciting arm of the service. Fast riding, dashing onsets, scouring the woods, all come in as a part of the skirmisher's duty. From that time till we reached Opelousas, we did not lose sight of the rear-guard of the retreating column. Every hour or two, they would make a stand, deliver a volley or two, and then ride with all their might for another covert. These Texans almost always dismount when they fire. Hiding their bodies behind their horses, they rest their guns in the saddles, and thus render our return-fire useless until they are mounted. Once we had a fine view of them. Some four or five hundred lingered by the edge of a thick wood, hoping to get a few chance shots at us. One of our Parrott guns was brought to bear on them; and, in a very few minutes, they concluded that in the woods was better than out of them. At another

time, we came suddenly upon a broad plain; and
on the farther side of it were some two thousand of
the foe, all mounted. We sat, and looked at them
for a little while; but, as our cannon had been mired
about a mile in the rear, we were unable to make
an attack. Our cavalry were itching for a charge;
but it was concluded best not to risk any thing:
so, after the interchange of some hundred or two
shots, they moved quietly away. Then the chase
began anew. Once only was the advance cavalry
taken by surprise. There is, close to the little
village of Opelousas, a dense wood. From information which we had gained, we felt sure that
there was no force in the thicket; and so rode leisurely on. When within about a hundred yards
of a covert, whiz, whiz, came the bullets, singing
around our heads. Only two of our boys tumbled
from their saddles; and these were killed instantly.
Of the two, one was a negro. He was acting as
guide; but was well armed, like the rest of the
cavalry. He was a brave fellow; and, when he
was struck, was in the van. I remained by his
side for some little time, anxious to see the effect
produced on the soldiers by the sight of death. I
had been talking with Porte Crayon, just before,
on this question. He surprised me by telling me
of the perfect indifference on such matters that
characterizes the soldier. He said, that, after the

battle of Antietam, the over-wearied boys laid down on the field, by the side of the killed, to sleep, and sometimes even used their dead comrades for pillows. One man he told me of, who brought his fiddle, which he had carried through the campaign, and, sitting down on the nearest dead body, began to play and sing. Indeed, there is no merrier time in the soldier's life than just before and just after a battle. When the wounded are brought into the surgeon's room, they are met by the jokes of their comrades, also wounded.

" Well, Jim, where did you get hit, old boy ? "

Jim grunts out, "The rascals took me in the hip ; and now I shall have to hobble all the rest of my days. Well, there's nothing like dying for one's country ! "

I stood by the dead soldier as our boys went by, and was struck by their cold indifference. Once in a while, I noticed a look of pity ; but, generally, the impulse to gaze was only curiosity.

" Look, Tom ! there's one covey gone. Say, they hit him right in the chops, didn't they ? "

It is not on the battle-field that soldiers recognize the solemnity of death. Then they are under the influence of excitement. But I have seen them affected to tears as they stood by the grave of a comrade ; and while I spoke to them of those far away, whose hearts would be stricken by the sad news, and of that other home, the soldier's home, where the good Father has a room in his great mansion for every true soul, they have been subdued, and even bowed down. A soldier, like a sailor, is a creature of impulse. His life makes him so. Every day is so full of uncertainty, that at length he feels that the immediate present alone is his; and he lives in it and enjoys it as best he can. *Your* days are like the links of a chain: this one presumes the next, and so on indefinitely. *His* days are all insulated. There is no necessary connection between to-day and to-morrow. He holds this hour firmly in his grasp: the next he may not be able to hold. So he grows reckless and careless.

After our column reached Opelousas, I left it, intending to go on with my work in the labor system; and I found but one thing, that, to my mind, marred the glory of our march through the Têche. That was the extensive system of plundering and pillaging which was carried on by the stragglers, — a class of men sufficiently large to attract attention. I afterwards found that their practices had been made known to the general, and that several of the offenders had been condemned to be shot. I am not one of those who would have mercy on a rebel; but even war is not exactly barbarism: it does not give a soldier license to do as he chooses with what does not belong to him. He has no right to enter a poor man's house, and, holding his pistol to his head, frighten him out of two hundred dollars in gold and silver, — his all. The soldier is hired to fight. If he is in the enemy's country, he should feed off and live on him: more than this he has no right to do. What is worst of all, this system of plundering demoralizes a force, and, in a short time, renders it ungovernable. Let it be known that the soldiers may leave the ranks at will, and in a short time you will have no men to command.

What made me more indignant was the fact, that the men who were bearing the brunt of the battle were not the ones who were enriching themselves. They simply hewed a way, through which others, less worthy, came at their leisure. The stragglers numbered not more than five hundred in all. These did all the mischief. One of these we found in the Newtown jail, with a thousand dollars in gold and silver on his person. If you should go up to any cottage within fifty miles of the rear, you would probably find some five or six of these fellows sitting in the gallery, smoking, sleeping, or boasting of their exploits. If you should take the trouble to empty their pockets, you would find an assortment of articles sufficiently large for a Jew to commence business with. They would show you

gold pencils, silver spoons, and large rolls of Confederate bills, and offer to sell you relics enough to
fill a good-sized museum.   There was an independence or an audacity about these fellows which was
very striking.   They would enter a house with the
air of one who owned the place, and order the land-
lord to prepare dinner for two or three, as the case
might be; and, while the frightened Creole was
hurrying and bustling to do their bidding, they were
quietly opening all his drawers, looking under his
beds, unlocking his trunks, and making whatever
discoveries they could.   Perhaps, by the time dinner
was announced, the whole party would have donned
a new suit of clothes; and, not satisfied with eating
the best the poor man had, would proceed to fill their
pockets with his watches, his wife's jewelry, and all
the little articles of *vertu* which could be found.   At
Franklin, Mr. Secesh and his family were quietly
seated at the breakfast-table.   Upon congratulating
himself, that, so far, his property had remained in-
tact, he saw half a dozen soldiers just entering his
gate.   They came very leisurely into the room
where he sat with his wife and children, and politely
requested them to rise from the table, and make
room for Uncle Sam's boys : then, after having
satisfied their hunger with what the planter had
supplied for himself, they pocketed every silver fork
and spoon, and as leisurely took their departure.   I

confess, that, in this particular instance, I heard Mr. Secesh whine about his trouble, with a great deal of inward chuckling. He was a bad man, a Northern man, an adventurer, who had married a large plantation, and out-Heroded Herod in his virulence against the Yankees.

But the practice I most deeply deplore. Once I came near getting into difficulty by trying to check it. I remained all night with a man who had suffered severely from these military thieves. About five o'clock in the morning, I was roused by a tremendous noise down stairs. Dressing myself with all due haste, I went to the window, and, looking down, saw one of the gang just emerging from the cellar window below, his arms and pockets full of plunder. Presenting my pistol to his *caput*, I demanded what he was doing. He turned suddenly, caught sight of the ugly little revolver close to his brains, and, with a rapidity only equalled by a turtle drawing in his head when struck, he tumbled back into the room, greatly surprised. I went to the door to find the rest of the gang, when I was met by the roundest and most complete cursing it has ever been my fortune to receive. Expletives which I had supposed were long since obsolete, and all the most damnatory phrases in our language, were used with refreshing license. The men had screened themselves on the other

side of a bayou; and, when I drew my weapon
on them, they dodged behind the levee, and
made good their escape. Just then, I recollected
that I was in my shirt-sleeves, and without any
insignia of rank, and started for the house to
get my coat. I had proceeded but a few steps,
however, when I found myself surrounded by five
of the gang, each with his musket. A pretty fix
to be in, surely! The rascals might shoot me, and
then swear that I was a planter who had offered
them violence. Nothing but the most unadulterated bravado would clear me. So, just as I
was pondering what it was best to do, the fellow
who had played the turtle so beautifully, quietly
cocked his musket, and said, —

"Throw down your pistol, or I will shoot!"

This, of course, was unendurable. My pistol
had on it the name of the friend who gave it to
me, and it was one of the last things to be given
up.

He repeated his very praiseworthy determination to shoot me; when I rather took him by surprise by bellowing in my loudest tones, —

"Sirrah, I place you under arrest; and, if you
budge an inch, you shall become intimately acquainted with that" (displaying my pistol to the
best possible advantage). "Shoulder arms!" I
repeated, as loud as I could bawl.

The fellow was completely disconcerted, and actually came to the shoulder arms; when I put on the coat I had sent for (having on shoulder-straps, of course), and placed the fellow under arrest. But I never preferred charges against him, and so the matter ended as a joke.

But, as a simple example of the impudence and daring of these stragglers, the anecdote serves its purpose.

There was one thing which aroused the just indignation of the army. It was the attempt of the inhabitants to deceive us. In some conspicuous place would be hung up the British flag, or the red, white, and blue of the pretended French population. Not once between Brashear City and Opelousas was the French or English flag waving in company with that of the United States. To my mind, they had no right to claim exemption from the ravages of war on the ground that they were British or French subjects. They were citizens of this country. Most of them had lived here from ten to twenty-five years. They had made their fortunes here, had married their wives here, and lived in luxuriant ease on the property of their wives, who were subject to the United-States Government and laws. By some quibble of international law, such beings may have the military right to claim protection; but their moral right is ex-

tremely doubtful. The property which has been
acquired under our Government ought not to be
held as secure and exempted from confiscation,
unless there are two flags, — the one proving allegiance to the British sovereign, and the other
showing respect for, and temporary allegiance to,
the United States. Our soldiers caught this idea
at once. They regarded the exhibition of a foreign
flag as a direct insult, and the inmates of such
houses had very little mercy shown them. I verily
believe, that, if a land-owner had hoisted the American flag, not a soldier would have touched his
property. It would have been held sacred by the
rudest of our boys. But the foreign flag seemed
defiant; and the men who raised it (in many cases,
they openly avowed their sympathy with the
South) were no more free than their neighbors
from violence done to themselves and their property. Nearly all the foreigners whom I have met
have been insulting cowards. They have spoken
against the "invaders," until compelled to silence
by direct order; and have, I am glad to say, suffered equal damage with those who were more
honest and more manly.

When I got back to the city, I heard the glorious rumor, that five hundred of our cavalry had
made their way through five hundred miles of
rebel territory, and were safely encamped just

beyond our pickets at Baton Rouge. There was a certain sonorousness and resonance to the rumor, that gave it the appearance of truth. It had not about it that dimness, vagueness, and bashfulness with which most of Madam Rumor's children make their appearance. It came rattling down on the ground in full armor, like a healthy, strong-limbed man. I shut myself up in my room for full an hour, wondering if it could be true; then rushed out to the St. Charles, looked on the book, and saw the name of Col. Grierson in good round characters. It was not a dream; and so, with a heart swelling with excitement, I cried out, "Eureka!" and rushed hither and thither, until I found the hero, whom I grasped by the hand as though he had been my brother. He had been through every conceivable danger. The enemy had sought to cut him off, first with five thousand men, and again with three thousand; but, with a rapidity which argued skill and daring, he made long circuits, and got free. He had as many as five skirmishes in the course of twenty-four hours. Several times he charged on superior forces, and scattered them. He confirmed, in the most assured manner, the opinions which I have already expressed concerning the strength of the Confederacy, and the feelings of certain classes of the people. He said, " The Confederacy is an empty shell. I was surprised at the appearance of things inside the ring. The strength of the rebels has been over-estimated. They have neither the armies nor the resources we have given them credit for. Passing through their country, I found thousands of good Union men, who are ready and anxious to return to their allegiance the moment they can do so with safety to themselves and families. They will rally round the old flag by scores, wherever our army advances. I could have brought away a thousand with me who were anxious to come, — men whom I found fugitives from their home, hid in the swamps and forests, where they were hunted like wild beasts, by the conscripting - officers, *with bloodhounds.*"

At Brookhaven, the citizens begged for paroles. At Louisville, every house was closed. The inhabitants had been told, that, if the Yankees should ever come, they would ravish their daughters, butcher their sons, and pillage their homes. When they were disabused of this idea, — of course, they were mostly poor Creoles, — they were profuse in their hospitalities, and in their expressions of a hope that the Union would be restored.

This was the testimony of all the officers. It proves what I have before asserted, — that this Rebellion originated only in the hearts of the large land-owners; that the humbler classes were won to acquiescence by bribes, threats, and vigilance committees; that to-day these same land-owners have lost their influence with the people, who see through the perfidy of their advisers, and are ready to welcome the flag of Washington to their hearts and homes.

The gallant colonel gave valuable evidence upon another subject. He has proved, beyond all doubt, the exceeding value of cavalry as a military arm. For some unaccountable reason, there has been a strong prejudice against it; and yet it has done more than any thing else to give the rebels their reputation for quick movements, surprises, and raids. There is an opinion abroad, that our army is naturally sluggish; that its chief characteristics are fortitude and patience; while the rebels, lacking in these qualities, make up for them by a certain genius for dash, which makes them a terrible foe. Wherever Stuart rides, he carries terror with him. His victories are half won before he strikes a blow. Our soldiers feel that he may pounce on them at any minute, and that he is resistless as a hawk in a fowl-yard. The rebels have done more to win respect for themselves by their cavalry raids than by all their infantry movements. Even in Europe, it is said that the South is brilliant, quick, daring even to recklessness;

while the North is cautious, slow, but ponderous. The criticism is a true one; but there is no need of its being so. We are not a slow people. We have all the elements of character necessary to brilliant movements largely developed. The little cavalry we have abundantly proves this. The rebels cannot show horsemen more tractable, firm, enduring, or skilful, than those of Magee or Barret, Williamson or Perkins. I have ridden with these men, and know how they handle themselves. They are ready for any service, and are most delighted when they have a chance to show their endurance. I saw Perkins, at Franklin, get off his horse, lie down on his back, have a bullet-wound in his leg dressed, mount his beast again, and dash into the woods, followed by his men with a wild hurrah! I have seen Williamson, when he had his hand badly wounded by a sabre, carry his company over the plain to flank the enemy, and drive them from their covert. I know it is said that Southerners are riders by nature; but there is a vast deal of sophistry in the remark. Our boys will ride at break-neck speed, feet out of the stirrups, swinging their swords in great and little circles, over ditches and through the woods, and into the midst of the enemy; and that is as good riding as you need for the cavalry service. Our cavalry horses, too, are vastly superior to those of the enemy generally. Northern horses will weigh, on an average, nine hundred pounds; while those of the Southerners, generally a cross between a Creole pony and what is called an American horse, will not average more than eight hundred pounds. In a charge, that hundred pounds is worth every thing. You have not merely impetuosity, but you have weight, which is a very important item. Let us get over this unfortunate prejudice; let us give the army its due proportion of cavalry, and allow it to make raids on the enemy; and our boys, I am sure, will carry terror wherever they go, and find their way into the remotest corners of the Confederacy, and take rough hold of its very heart.

Why, neither Morgan with all his boasted exploits, nor Stuart, nor Wheeler, can tell a story that will compare in heroism with that of Col. Grierson. They never traversed five hundred miles of our country, — a large stint for sixteen days, — doing injury which cannot be repaired in three months. What they have done is child's play by the side of this.

The moral effect of Grierson's exploit must be tremendous; yet it is only one of a long series of exploits which our boys are all ready to achieve. All they ask is permission, and in a wonderfully short time they will so harass and terrify the infantry of the enemy, — tearing up the railroads,

24

destroying their telegraphs, seizing their commissary-stores, — that they will fly to their homes
in dismay. It is in the Northern heart to do this.
Grierson has commenced: Magee and Perkins and
Williamson are ready to carry it on.

The army was afterwards, a second time, taken
to Port Hudson. It had been promised to the nine-
months' men, that they should return to their homes
in August *viâ* the Mississippi River. All of us
hoped the promise might prove a prophecy; but
few had any faith in it. During the first few
months of sixty-three, we all (I mean the whole
North) lived on faith alone. We knew that we
were in the right; that our cause claimed the help
of the Almighty; and that, some time, — Heaven
alone knew when, — we should see light. It was
a dark, dreary time. The Potomac Army had
crossed the Rappahannock, and, under glorious Joe
Hooker, was going straight into Richmond; when
the rebel force met it, threw it into confusion, and
added another to its numberless retreats. It seems
to be a doomed force. Its officers are as brave and
as skilful as those of any other *corps d'armée ;* its
men are the very flower of the land; their courage
has never been impeached: still they have, in the
last two years, done little else than check the raids
of the enemy, and keep Washington from being
captured.

I should like to whisper into your ear, by way of parenthesis, that, if some serious accident should happen to the telegraph-wire between Washington and the headquarters of the Potomac Army (and by this time it must be terribly tangled, if we judge by the contradictory messages it has carried), the Eastern force would at once accomplish some brilliant achievement. Interference is the grand cause of failure. Shut up a few officials I could name, and Richmond will be ours within thirty days.

In the West, nothing had been done. Rosecrans, Grant, Burnside, had been busy enough, but had effected nothing. We were at a stand-still all over the country. Thoughtful men began to ask, "How long will the people bear this silence, which seems so like defeat, and not murmur?" And yet, be it said to the praise of the people, there was no sign of misgiving on the part of the North: it still gave its treasure and its sons.

Those months were the dark hour before the dawn. We knew it not then; but so it proved.

When our boys invested Port Hudson, they had, most of them, been in the Têche for a month; and, having started in light marching order, were without change of clothing. Yet they were uniformly cheerful, enduring the fatigues and deprivations of the campaign like veterans. They had no tents, and, for a long while, no meat; nothing but coffee and hard-tack.

Our position was on the further edge of a heavily wooded lot; and our line, shutting the rebel works in, was about seven miles long. On the river-side, the enemy's position was so fortified by nature, that no number of gunboats could hope to capture it. On the land-side, it was protected by a high parapet, in front of which was a ditch about twenty feet wide and six feet deep. Between our position and theirs was what looked to be a plain, three-quarters of a mile wide; but, when examined by the proper officers, it was found to be full of deep ravines, at the bottom of which was broken timber, and very tall, dense chaparral. Under proper circumstances (i.e., with a good supply of provisions and ammunition and twenty-five thousand men), it could resist any force we could bring against it.

We made some assaults; but they were soon found to be of little use. We could not get near enough to the enemy to make a dash over the parapet. We had to grope our way through deep ravines, or slowly find it under and over fallen timber. A regiment could not march in line, on account of the thick chaparral, brier-bushes, and gullies. We then sat down quietly, to starve the rebels out, and to harass them by our artillery practice. We fenced them in with our guns some six weeks before they cried, "Enough!"

It was very interesting to go along our line, and note the little events which history will think too trivial to mention. I spent a few hours with the Zouaves, who seem to be as wild and willing a set of men as any in the army. Their sharpshooters went out every night, carrying twenty-four-hours' rations; and, hiding behind some providential hillock, would watch eagerly till some unfortunate head was lifted above the parapet, when whiz would go a bullet. Fortunate was the aforementioned head, if it could open its eyes to the world again. Some of our sharpshooters crawled up to within a hundred, and even eighty, yards of the parapet; and, all day, the constant crack of the rifle announced that some one unfortunate had put himself in a dangerous place.

The rebels, too, were good shots. There was one man who was a source of great annoyance to us; and many a poor fellow will testify to his existence by showing a very peculiar and ugly wound in leg or arm. He used a double-barreled shot-gun, of English make, with a bore large enough to admit a ball weighing an ounce and a half. The bullets he used were double the size of those made for the Enfield rifle. He covered himself with the long moss which hung from the branches of every tree;

and, climbing some forty feet up a sturdy cypress, could get a fine view of many of the sharpshooters, and even of the boys in the most advanced batteries. We never could tell in which tree he was, though we were constantly on the watch for him; and yet, if you chanced to show your head over the cotton-bales, which were our fortifications, you would be reminded of the necessity of prudence by a distinct hum which is a very unpleasant sound to hear. He disabled men standing more than three-quarters of a mile off. I do not know that he actually killed any one at that distance; but he made some very disagreeable wounds.

One of our men was captured by a very neat piece of strategy. About a hundred and fifty yards in front of one of our regiments was a spring of clear cold water. After having drunk the vile fluid which oozes through a clay bank, oftentimes impregnated with a very disagreeable odor, and always having the appearance of mud paste (being chiefly composed of that very necessary but not always palatable substance), the boys were willing to run some little risk for the sake of a draft of genuine water. One day, a sick man asked his chum to fill his canteen. Without hesitation, he promised to do so; and so, crawling up with all due caution, he at last reached the spring. It so happened, however, that a rebel sharpshooter had seen him. He waited quietly till the canteen was filled; and then, drawing a bead on the soldier, cried out, —

"I say, Yank!"

The startled Unionist at once saw his predicament, and began to think that his last minute had come. He at last got voice enough to cry out, —

"Well, what do you want?"

"Want you. Walk over this way, please."

"It was certainly a very courteous invitation, and there seemed no way to avoid accepting it; for the rebel kept him covered with his rifle. He was in an unpleasant predicament; and, when the rebel had enjoyed his embarrassment long enough, he cried out, —

"I say, Yank, aren't you coming? or shall I send some lead after you?"

This was a very pointed remark. Nothing was left the poor Unionist but to obey; and so, with unwilling steps, he walked over to the jocose rebel, and gave himself up.

I spent a couple of hours very pleasantly behind a four-gun battery, which delivered its fire every ten minutes throughout the day. Its business was to dismount one of the enemy's pieces on the works immediately opposite. The rebels worked their gun very defiantly for a long while (for it is very difficult to hit within a circle five feet in diameter, a mile distant); but, at length, a well-directed ball sent clouds of dust into the air, and scattered the gunners, who did not return during the day. Along the entire line, such work as this was being done every hour. We must have thrown many tons of iron, which was expected to harass the enemy rather than do him immediate harm. It was a long, tedious, and dreary work to capture the place. Disease at length got into the ranks, and made sad havoc with the men. Every day, loads of sick went to the hospital. Thither I followed, in my turn, to study the character and test the skill of the army-surgeon; and, I must confess, I have not been more disappointed in any body of officers. That there are good surgeons, kind-hearted, considerate, patriotic men, in our regiments, I will not doubt; I know some such: but that a large number (shall I say a large majority?) are men who took to the army because they could not make a living in the country town from which they came, or because, being young, their blunders can be more easily hidden there than anywhere else, I do most seriously aver. While lying on my blanket (our hospital was a cotton-shed, a roof only), I watched the M.D. as he went the grand round among his patients. His attendant carried some quinine powders in one hand, and a large box of blue pills in the other. The first patient received a blue pill, the second a quinine powder, the next a blue pill, and so on; the one medicine alternating with the other, until the whole number had been prescribed for. The next morning, the first patient, who had the day before swallowed a blue pill, received a quinine powder; and the next one, who had been regaled with a quinine powder, received a blue pill; and so on, again, to the end of the row. As I turned over, and groaned, wondering which of those two diabolical medicines it would be my lot to gulp down, I could not help wondering at the flexibility of a surgeon's conscience; while, at the same time, my wonder at the mortality in the army ceased.

It was a grand day, — the glorious old Fourth of July, — when a strange steamer came bowling down the river, bringing the unexpected but glorious news of the fall of Vicksburg. When it was announced, the whole line sent up its joy in many a ringing hurrah and many a silent prayer. The news reached Gen. Gardner's ears, and he at once sent to Banks to know if it was true. Our general sent back a copy of the official despatch from Grant, and that day Port Hudson changed hands. Gardner said, "If Vicksburg has fallen, it is of no use for me to hold out longer." I have no doubt that the rebel officers were dismayed; but I have very good authority for believing that the rank and file were glad enough to end their war experiences then and there. They were poorly clothed, having on no uniform, — nothing but the rude, home-made clothes of the South, — and had been for some time on short rations. They had been deserting in large numbers for many days, and were doubtless glad to be freed from the conscription-act, and from imperilling their lives for the sake of the slave-holders.

On the 8th of July, the Mississippi was opened from the Passes to Cairo, the Confederacy was cut in two, and the 'rebel cause received a blow from which it will never recover.

The dawn has come after patient waiting. When will the " perfect day " come ?

THE END.

Printed by John Wilson and Son, Boston.

INDEX

299

DATE DUE

NOV 25 '85			
GAYLORD			PRINTED IN U.S.A.